FIGHTING
BULLIES

The Case for a Career in
Plaintiffs' Law

WILLIAM T. REID, IV

"*Fighting Bullies* is a compelling and timely call to service through the practice of law. This book will serve as an essential guide that offers powerful reasons to pursue the path of a plaintiffs' lawyer. Drawing on a distinguished career and a deep well of personal experience, Reid shows how this work not only leads to professional success but also provides the opportunity to make a lasting difference—by standing up for individuals and protecting their rights."

—Ben Barnes, Former Lieutenant Governor of Texas

"If Hunter S. Thompson ever wrote a book on law, this would be that book."

—Anonymous Yale Law Professor

"*Fighting Bullies* is a rich read and its message is profound: The most important career decision for any lawyer, young or old, is to find what you love and do it with all your heart. This book is a testament to a lawyer who refused to take the traditional road and, because of it, is a singular force for good in the modern world."

—William Taylor III, Founding Partner of Zuckerman Spaeder and One of the Country's Foremost Trial Lawyers

"I love this book. I wish I could give a powerful testimonial because it's all true, but it would be career suicide … I'm going to give it to all my friends."

—Anonymous BigLaw Partner

"*Fighting Bullies* is a tour de force. Reid shows how the courtroom can be a battleground for justice, and how the right kind of lawyer can change not only lives, but the face of the world. For anyone considering law school—or wondering what kind of lawyer they want to be—this is a must-read."

—Wayne Reaud, Nationally Recognized Icon of the Plaintiffs' Bar and Founding Partner of Reaud, Morgan & Quinn

"A thoughtful and provocative look at why law students and young lawyers tend to not be professionally satisfied and how to fix it. A must-read for those in search of positive direction in the law!"

—SHANIN SPECTER, COFOUNDING PARTNER OF KLINE & SPECTER, PC, AND PROFESSOR OF PRACTICE, UC LAW SAN FRANCISCO

"Bill Reid has a great deal of wisdom to provide to any aspiring young lawyer. I recommend that anyone headed into a legal career pay very close attention."

—MARK HOLLIDAY, NATIONALLY KNOWN LITIGATION TRUSTEE

"Reid is a trailblazer in plaintiffs' law and his book displays his passion for the law. You can do no wrong in paying heed to some of the advice he has on this career path."

—KENNETH KRYS, FOUNDER AND EXECUTIVE CHAIRMAN, KRYS GLOBAL

"Bill Reid has redefined the art of what is possible when it comes to examining how to prosecute large-scale complex commercial disputes."

—PETER KRAVITZ, FOUNDING PRINCIPAL OF PROVINCE FIRM

"Bill is an exuberant evangelist for plaintiffs' work. All law students should get *Fighting Bullies* as assigned reading before they take a summer job."

—LEE RUDY, PLAINTIFFS' SECURITIES CLASS ACTION LAWYER, KESSLER TOPAZ MELTZER & CHECK, LLP

"*Fighting Bullies* is a must-read for young lawyers wanting to do something meaningful with their careers, separate and apart from merely chasing money."

—MIKAL WATTS, MASS TORT LAWYER, FOUNDER OF WATTS LAW FIRM

"*Fighting Bullies* is a must-read for aspiring lawyers and lawyers in Big Law practices. In a colorful style, Bill describes the key mentors who guided his career, his major victories, the virtues of plaintiffs' trial work, and excellent strategies to build a cohesive trial team. Finally, he sends warning signals about the proliferation of AI in law practice and the risk to Big Law."

—Marc Kirschner, National Bankruptcy Trustee, Teneo

"*Fighting Bullies* is a must-read not only for any law student but for all the lawyers out there who are stuck in BigLaw jobs. Bill Reid isn't just talking—he's been walking the walk for more than two decades. We'll be sending a copy of this book to everyone we interview from now on."

—Bradley Beckworth, Trial Lawyer, Nix Patterson, LLP

"*Fighting Bullies* provides a sorely needed counterweight against the biases of law school and the legal profession, which too often push the best and brightest into careers of heartbreaking toil and burnout. Bill Reid provides a living example of how to take a more fulfilling path, to fight for what's right while prospering financially and raising a family."

—Tucker Ronzetti, Trial and Appellate Lawyer

"Bill Reid's *Fighting Bullies* is required reading for anyone interested in becoming a lawyer—or better still a happy and successful lawyer. He adroitly illustrates how law schools feed their best and brightest to the world's biggest law firms, resulting in broken dreams of too many aspiring lawyers. And he proposes a better way—one that he took."

—Katrina Dewey, CEO and Founder of Lawdragon

"For over a decade I have watched Mr. Reid take on the biggest and baddest bullies on the planet. Bill has defeated them with endless hard work, tireless enthusiasm, boundless hope, and a wonderful sense of humor. His creativity, expertise, and fearless dedication to fighting these bullies is only surpassed by his success as a husband, father, and colleague."

—Scott Ellington, Former Chief Legal Officer of
Highland Capital Management

"Bill and his colleagues have earned the respect of the defense bar because they live by the motto 'fight hard but fight fair.'"

—MICHAEL B. CARLINSKY, GLOBAL CO-MANAGING PARTNER AND HEAD OF
COMPLEX LITIGATION OF QUINN EMANUEL URQUHART & SULLIVAN, LLP

"As a thirty-plus-year plaintiffs'-side lawyer and law firm founder, I wish that I had this book when I was in law school."

—ADAM J. LEVITT, FOUNDING PARTNER, DiCELLO LEVITT, LLP

"Every accomplished plaintiffs' lawyer has a story for how they became a plaintiffs' lawyer. Why? Because very few started out as plaintiffs' lawyers. Until now."

—SHAWN RABIN, TRIAL LAWYER, PARTNER, SUSMAN GODFREY

"Thank goodness Bill wrote this book. It should be required reading for anyone who went to law school with the goal of improving our society. This book proves that you can do well financially without compromising your values."

—JASON ITKIN, TRIAL LAWYER, ARNOLD & ITKIN

"This book should be in every 1L's 'go bag.' And if you should ever find yourself facing a bully...call Bill."

—TODD SNYDER, GLOBAL CO-HEAD OF RESTRUCTURING
AND REORGANIZATION AT PIPER SANDLER, TRS ADVISORS

WREN HOUSE
press

For permission requests, please contact:
Wren House Press
www.wrenhousepress.com

eBook ISBN: 978-1-967115-16-7
Paperback ISBN: 978-1-967115-17-4
Hardcover ISBN: 978-1-967115-18-1
Audiobook ISBN: 978-1-967115-19-8

Printed in the United States of America
First Edition
Book design and cover art by Erin Tyler.

To Judge Reynaldo G. Garza

There's no other way to say it: You changed my life. You gave me a shot, took me out of the only world I knew in the Northeast, and brought me to Texas.

What you gave me wasn't just a clerkship—it was a PhD in law and life.

Rarely a day goes by when I don't plagiarize your quips, retell your stories, or rely upon your wisdom. You have left an indelible impression on me.

I constantly rely upon your basic framework for how to approach any case, which boils down to the very basics of right and wrong. You taught me to focus on these equities in every case, and I've never let it go.

This book is my attempt to pass on just some of what you gave to me. It's the best career and life advice I can offer, because it's built on the foundation you laid.

This Book Might Change Your Life

I F I'D READ THIS BOOK while I was in law school, I'd be a lawyer today.

I graduated from Duke Law School in 2001, when the BigLaw chokehold on top law schools was tight. Like most law students, I believed I had only two options:

1. I COULD DO "MEANINGFUL" public interest work, but make little money and live my life in perpetual debt, or,

2. I COULD TAKE A "BIGLAW" JOB, make a ton of money, but not do important (or interesting) work.

I was twenty-three (and an idiot) when I was in law school, so I picked BigLaw, because I liked money and thought lots of money would make me happy, even if the actual work was not something I cared much about.

I summered at Fenwick & West, one of the premier Silicon Valley firms. I picked them because at the time, they were billed as a good lifestyle firm in the BigLaw world, and I figured I could get the best of both worlds.

I HATED IT.

It was obvious—literally in the first week—that working in BigLaw meant I was a meaningless cog in a lifeless machine that churned out pointless paperwork. It felt like nothing I did mattered to an actual person—because it didn't.

I'd already decided I wasn't OK with being poor just to do "meaningful" public interest work, and because I thought these were my only options, I believed I had to leave the legal profession (so I did that, in a very emotionally unhealthy way, blowing up my life and career and eventually getting fired from Fenwick & West. I tell that story in detail in my book *I Hope They Serve Beer In Hell*).

I met Bill Reid about a decade ago, and quickly realized that my narrow view of possible legal career paths was wrong. There *is* a path to do meaningful work in law, *and* to do well financially:

Plaintiffs' law.

The only thing I knew about plaintiffs' lawyers in law school was they were ambulance chasers (and the ones you see on TV and billboards mostly are). To me, this path wasn't even a consideration.

But I had no idea that there were other types of plaintiffs' lawyers, and that people like Bill Reid existed. People who take on huge companies that commit illegal and immoral acts against regular people and beat them in court.

People that fight bullies and make lots of money doing it.

It's not just Bill and his firm that do this, of course. There are so many plaintiffs' lawyers that do incredible work, and Bill details many of them in this book.

But I had no idea about any of them. No one told me, and truthfully, I didn't do enough of my own research to realize it (which is my fault, of course).

I'm not saying the sort of work plaintiffs' lawyers do is necessarily "better." For some people, public interest or BigLaw are the best option, and that's fine.

But if you're like me, and want both meaningful work and financial reward, there's a better option: become a plaintiffs' lawyer and take on high-profile, complex litigation cases where the only way justice can be served is through the tort system.

What I also like about this book is that Bill states his case up front: He believes being a plaintiffs' lawyer is the best possible path to a meaningful legal career. He doesn't pretend he's objective. He tells you what he thinks and where his biases lie, and shows you where the skeletons in the closet are—even for his side.

That's why I'm excited to write this foreword. Had this book existed in 2001, I truly think it would have led me to a meaningful and fruitful career in plaintiffs' law.

For many of you, it's not too late to do exactly that.

TUCKER MAX
JUNE 2025

PART 1:

The Truth About Law School, Campus Interviewing, and BigLaw

Chapter 1

Setting the Record Straight

E VERYTHING YOU'VE BEEN TOLD about being a lawyer is wrong. If you're an ambitious young lawyer who wants to do good in the world— and do well financially—you should seriously consider plaintiffs' law.

I know you're probably thinking: *Everyone knows the money comes from BigLaw and the impact comes from public interest work.*

Yes, you were told that. I was even told that when I went to law school a hundred years ago.

But let me ask you a question: *What if everything you've been told about the legal profession is wrong?*

Maybe "wrong" is too strong. Maybe you've been told only a fraction of what you need to know to make an informed career choice.

Here's the truth: *Law school does a poor job of showing you all of your career options, including what I believe is the best option... becoming a plaintiffs' lawyer.*

Law professors on average practiced law for just 3.7 years, which means most of them never had enough experience to understand and then teach others about the real-world practice of law. They're not able to guide you on a career path because most of them never traveled on one. Without substantial real-world experience, their career advice is necessarily limited and woefully incomplete.

Law schools today are not much different than when I went to school over thirty years ago. They're very good at teaching theory, but they don't do a good job of giving you the knowledge to choose a career path. Which means that you, just like me, will have to figure all of this out for yourself.

And the stakes are real:

If you get it wrong, you'll spend 80,000 to 100,000 hours trapped in a career you hate.

If you get it right, you will spend your life doing work you love.

THE REAL COST OF CHOOSING THE
WRONG CAREER PATH

The mental health consequences of getting it wrong are severe. Lawyering is among the most stressful jobs there are. On average, American lawyers rate their career happiness at 2.6/5, which puts it in the bottom 7 percent of all US careers.

According to the American Bar Association (ABA), lawyers experience depression at rates 3.6 times higher than the general population. Other studies indicate that lawyers have a depression rate of between 28 and 46 percent—compared to 6.7 percent for all other US careers.

Many resort to substance abuse to cope. In a 2016 study by the ABA, it was reported that between 21 and 36 percent of lawyers qualify as "problem drinkers." In contrast, the general population has a problem-drinking rate of approximately 8 to 10 percent.

Suicide rates are even more alarming. The ABA reports that 11.4 percent of all lawyers have experienced suicidal thoughts. Other studies show that *suicide rates among American lawyers are six times higher* than the general population.

Bottom line: If you choose the wrong path you're either going to burn out, quit practicing law altogether ... or worse.

So ask: ***Don't you owe it to yourself to do the work necessary to find the best legal career path for you?***

QUESTIONS TO ASK YOURSELF TO DETERMINE YOUR IDEAL CAREER PATH

As you consider your career, ask yourself some general questions:

- Would you rather represent plaintiffs, or defendants?
- Would you rather seek justice, or deny it?
- Would you rather fight for David, or defend Goliath?
- Would you rather choose your battles, or have them assigned to you?

Let's get specific. Would you rather:

- Prosecute greedy fraudsters, or defend them?
- Hold polluters accountable, or shield them from liability?
- Take on deadly drug manufacturers, or protect them from lawsuits?
- Fight for victims, or for the corporations that harmed them?
- Hold the rich and powerful accountable, or protect and enable them?
- Build a career you're proud of, or just collect a paycheck?

I never even thought to ask myself these questions, and no one suggested that I ask them either.

That's why I wrote this book. Because you need to ask yourself questions like these in order to find your way.

I think there's a better path, but you've never been told about it.

For many of you, ***the best answer to these questions is a career in plaintiffs' law.***

Why is plaintiffs' law portrayed so negatively?

Because it serves powerful interests to keep it that way.

The "tort reform" movement, fueled by tobacco companies in the 1980s, then joined by corporate giants (like Dow Corning), has spent decades making people believe that American courts are flooded with frivolous lawsuits and runaway jury verdicts.

Tort reform isn't the product of neutral scholarship; it's the product of corporate money and self-interest. I'm going to call it what it is: *propaganda*.

More recently, the Chambers of Commerce spent millions pushing the same message: Plaintiffs' lawyers are greedy. The system is broken. The courts need protection—not from fraud, but from ordinary citizens seeking justice.

And it's worked.

Tort reform has led to changes in laws across the country—limiting liability, capping damages, and rigging the system against regular people. Today, billionaires like Elon Musk have pushed to change laws in Delaware and elsewhere to shield themselves from liability for their own self-dealing.

And along the way, it's poisoned the public perception of plaintiffs' lawyers as well.

How law schools are complicit in this portrayal of plaintiffs' law

But why do law schools, of all places, passively reinforce this narrative? Why do they create the impression that BigLaw is sophisticated and plaintiffs' law is second class?

The answer is simple—it benefits them:

- Law schools gain nothing by promoting plaintiffs' law (at least so far),
- BigLaw jobs boost job placement stats and rankings, and

- Very few law professors have had meaningful private practice—let alone a career as a plaintiffs' lawyer.

Law schools' rankings depend heavily on job placement and starting salary. If a school places you into a high-paying job, it looks like they've done their job, regardless of whether you find meaning or long-term happiness there. In fact, *U.S. News & World Report* now even publishes separate rankings based on how many graduates each law school sends to BigLaw.

All of this incentivizes law schools to promote BigLaw. Placement into BigLaw has become a badge of honor for law schools—and a marketing tool.

Meanwhile, because many academics and law school administrators negatively view plaintiffs' law, they are not interested in promoting a career that they see as subpar and second-rate. But they know virtually nothing about what a career in plaintiffs' law actually entails.

Maybe—and I'll admit this is speculation—some of the brightest BigLaw lawyers who didn't enjoy private practice ended up in academia. And maybe—just maybe— many smart plaintiffs' lawyers never became professors because they actually liked the work they were doing.

Regardless, the result is the same. Law schools often encourage their students to travel down the BigLaw conveyor belt. It's the path of least resistance, for both the students and the schools.

But what about you? Are you like Tucker, my friend who wrote the foreword to this book—someone who could have been a great plaintiffs' lawyer, but was never even told about it?

Think about that for a moment. Law schools should be helping you discover where *you* fit best in the legal world. Instead, whether purposely or through inertia, they're steering you to where it benefits *them* most.

Are you ready to explore this new path?

I'll show you why plaintiffs' law is not just a viable career option—but arguably the *best* option for ambitious young lawyers who want to pursue a career in litigation, achieve real impact, and accomplish real success.

I will tell you the stories of those who made the leap, including me—from BigLaw associates suffocating under billable hour quotas to building careers we could be proud of:

- Choosing our own clients
- Picking our own battles
- Fighting for causes that are actually worth it

You'll see how we took control of our futures, fought for the right causes, and found success beyond what we thought possible.

Most importantly, you'll get a road map for how to do the same.

You don't have to choose between making a difference and making a living.

Plaintiffs' law offers both.

CHAPTER 2

What Law School Won't Tell You (and Why)

THE MOMENT YOU BEGIN LAW SCHOOL, you are unwittingly stepping onto a conveyor belt. The entire legal education system will push you in a certain direction. Unless you are informed enough to recognize how the OCI (on-campus interview) system pushes you in a specific direction, you may find yourself deep in a legal career you never truly wanted. For the uninitiated, OCI is the annual process where prospective employers come in droves to interview law students for summer clerkships and full-time jobs.

LAW SCHOOL TEACHES THEORY, NOT CAREER PATHS

Law schools teach theory exceptionally well. But most do not prepare you for the real world, much less show you what kind of lawyer you could be.

How could this be?

For most of American history, the path to becoming a lawyer was straightforward: You apprenticed under a practicing attorney. You worked side by side with someone who had built a real-world legal practice. When you were ready, you took the bar exam, and if you passed, you were licensed to practice law. John Marshall, Abraham

Lincoln, Clarence Darrow, and countless others followed this model. They learned by observing real cases, meeting actual clients, and navigating the real-world practice of law at the hip of a very experienced lawyer.

Over the past century, law schools replaced apprenticeship with a purely academic model. The story of the transition to the academic model from the apprentice model is long and beyond the scope of this book. The truth is this: Law schools have always been designed to teach legal theory and create legal scholars, and have *never* been intended as trade schools to teach practical legal application.

You can spend three years in law school, and hundreds of thousands of dollars, studying legal theory. But when you graduate, you still have to take a separate, expensive bar review class just to pass the bar. And, of course, passing the bar does not mean that you are remotely equipped to represent a client.

Most law professors barely practiced law

Part of the reason that law schools don't spend time teaching you about the actual practice of law or about your legal career options is because, in most cases, **no one at the law school has substantive experience practicing actual law.**

According to the *Journal of Legal Education*, based on a study of the top twenty-six law schools, the average legal experience of law professors before entering academia is approximately 3.7 years. If you look closely at most law school professors' real-world experience, you'll find their limited professional experience is overwhelmingly rooted in BigLaw. And almost none of the tenured faculty at any law school were plaintiffs' lawyers in a commercial practice.

REGARDLESS OF THEIR PAST ROLES, ALMOST ALL LAW PROFESSORS SPENT VERY LITTLE TIME PRACTICING LAW.

And when it comes to career development offices, the situation is often worse. In my experience, most law school career development staff have even less practical experience than the faculty. Some career development officers moved straight from graduating law school into career development. No, really, this is a thing. Some law schools hire their unemployable graduates to pad their employment stats for law school rankings.

WHAT QUALIFIES SOMEONE WITH LITTLE OR NO REAL-WORLD LEGAL EXPERIENCE TO OFFER MEANINGFUL CAREER ADVICE?

You can't really blame law schools for failing students when it comes to career guidance. When you have no real-life legal experience, how much career wisdom do you truly have to offer? In sum, law school professors are really good at teaching you legal theory, but they are not able to give you much insight as to how it applies in the real world, much less how to think about your career.

THIS BOOK IS THE MISSING MANUAL ABOUT THE BEST LEGAL CAREER PATH

As a law student in the 1990s, I found little guidance to help shape a thoughtful pursuit of a legal career. Surely, there must be better guidance now, right?

Not really. Today, the world has changed and there is a lot more information online and in social media about law school—reliable and otherwise—but very little about career options.

When I was in school, the two leading books about law school were both based at Harvard Law School: *One L* by Scott Turow and *The Paper Chase* by John Jay Osborn, Jr. Those books really exaggerated the Harvard Law School experience and glorified the stereotypical mean law professor.

THEY FOCUSED ALMOST ENTIRELY ON THE LAW STUDENT EXPERI-ENCE—NOT ON PRACTICING LAW—JUST LIKE LAW SCHOOL ITSELF.

Since then, there has been a flood of books about going to law school and becoming a lawyer, including *The Happy Lawyer* by Nancy Levit and Douglas O. Linder, *Law School Confidential* by Robert H. Miller, and *Don't Go to Law School (Unless)* by Paul Campos. Today, there is more guidance about succeeding in law school and becoming a lawyer than my generation got. But these books do not help you in planning a meaningful career.

Most advice about law school and legal careers makes the same mistake: It treats success as landing the highest-paying job out of the gate—usually in BigLaw.

But BigLaw is not the only path, and for most, not even the best path.

How can you choose an area of practice without having any experience?

At medical school, students go through mandatory rotations in four chosen practice areas before they choose what to specialize in. There's no equivalent to a rotation at law school. Students are not exposed to different career paths—and again, the ones available at OCI are primarily BigLaw careers.

OCI is the annual process where law firms and other legal employers come directly to law school campuses to interview students for summer associate positions and full-time jobs. And BigLaw is exactly what it sounds like: the largest law firms in the country (or even the world). Their names become familiar to students from law school, where they sponsor events and facilities and turn up like clockwork at OCI to grab the best students for themselves.

There is no chance for law students to see what they might prefer from even the broadest range of options. Not only do students fail to appreciate many of these options, but the systemic bias toward BigLaw means *they might not even realize that many of these options exist*—because very few of these other employers turn up at OCI.

From a student's point of view, if you do not know the choices, how do you choose the first steps in your career? And once you choose your path, it's difficult to pivot.

In short, law school doesn't teach you how to build a legal career—it just sets you up to be recruited by BigLaw.

You can't make a smart career decision without understanding the system you're in. So let's talk about how that system really works.

CHAPTER 3

How Law Schools Push
You to BigLaw

O NE OF THE BIGGEST FORCES locking students into BigLaw isn't the classroom—it's OCI, the recruiting machine that law schools use as the primary means by which to help students meet potential employers.

MOST LAW STUDENTS DON'T CHOOSE BIGLAW;
IT GETS CHOSEN FOR THEM.

Law schools do not overtly send students to BigLaw. They are more subtle—they just push their students to attend OCI.

At every step along the way, every resource placed in front of law students, from the career development department, to OCI, to the advice given by their professors—all points in the same direction: BigLaw. Meanwhile, many students believe that OCI is the exclusive avenue to finding a job. They assume that all of their career options are available at OCI.

But most students are oblivious to the numerous problems with OCI.

First, most law schools do not actively try to recruit a variety of non-BigLaw firms to attend OCI. Of course, smaller firms like mine choose not to attend OCI because we do not hire enough people to justify the time and expense of sending someone there. Whether or not they stack the deck when it comes to OCI, law schools know that it does not provide their students with all of the available career options. They know it's largely a BigLaw feeding ground.

Second, law schools accommodate the legion of BigLaw employers and set up OCI to give them an advantage. They permit BigLaw to dictate when OCI occurs, which normally means BigLaw gets a first crack at hiring the students. It is now common for OCI to precede the traditional fall 2L hiring season for public interest employers and smaller firms in general. Then, after law schools set up OCI to give BigLaw priority access to students, they direct their students to attend OCI under the implicit assumption that all potential career paths are available.

No one tells the students that the overwhelming majority of firms participating in OCI are BigLaw. Nor does anyone tell students that there are BigLaw alternatives outside of OCI.

This means that the majority of law students attend OCI *before* they consider any other career options. No one gives students a full picture of their options so they can attend OCI with open eyes. Thus, once they arrive at OCI most students are vulnerable to the BigLaw trap, which, of course, is baited with a high starting salary.

Unless a student reads this book, has a good mentor, or otherwise figures out that the OCI game is rigged toward BigLaw, then they will have no idea to look beyond OCI—much less to consider looking for a plaintiffs' firm.

OCI IS A CONVEYOR BELT TO BigLaw

I call it the conveyor belt. Just as a factory sends a stream of homogenous products down a conveyor belt to satisfy the mass market, so too law school sends legions of uninformed students down the OCI conveyor belt to BigLaw—and the conveyor belt starts running the first day of law school. New students are taught to believe that the goal of law school is to get a BigLaw job. With a BigLaw job, they will get paid a ton, pay off their debts, and learn how to be a lawyer, then they'll do whatever they want.

BigLaw's Merit Filter Has Moved From Law School to the First Few Years of Your Career

In order to get a BigLaw job in the 1990s, a candidate had to demonstrate academic success. There were very few 1L jobs and the whole game was landing a 2L summer job. Back then was not much different than today: Everyone viewed landing a BigLaw job as the goal. The earliest OCI began in August and continued into the fall of a student's 2L year. BigLaw firms were more selective and they demanded that applicants provide full first-year grades, demonstrate academic success, and send writing samples and references. At my school, if you weren't in the top 20 percent or on Law Review you had little chance of a BigLaw job.

Now, in many cases, OCI occurs before first-year grades have even been published or Law Review elections held. BigLaw has abandoned the merit-based approach of the past because the qualifications are no longer as important.

It appears as though BigLaw now makes its merit selections during the first few years of an associate's career during the time when the majority of an incoming class leaves anyway.

BigLaw Has Overwhelming Influence at Law Schools

BigLaw has real power in law schools because they recruit big numbers. Many AmLaw 200 firms hire 50 to 100 associates a year (and, in some cases, many more). In fact, Paul Weiss hired 184 lawyers in its 2024 associate class.

A law school administrator recently observed about the behemoth law firm Kirkland & Ellis: "We have about fifteen students per year go to them. That means over the three classes we have right now, almost fifty students will end up at Kirkland. That gives Kirkland real power on our campus."

BigLaw helps law schools employ large numbers of their graduates, and employment percentage is a big factor in law school rankings. Even though the rankings are really just marketing, law schools are fixated on rankings because students are fixated on them.

BigLaw needs law students, and they aim to be the exclusive option for most of them. All of these tools are intended to limit a law student's options and force them into the BigLaw vortex.

BigLaw frequently requires exclusivity from its summer clerks. This means that many firms require that a student commit to work solely for a given law firm. As a result, students can't sample alternative firms. And it virtually ensures that a summer clerk will accept a job offer from a given firm because it's likely the only option they have.

BigLaw sometimes incentivizes 1L summer clerks with bonuses and extra pay in exchange for an agreement that the student spend the entire 2L summer with them as well. This adds to the exclusivity tool in further limiting a student's options.

Additionally, BigLaw has gotten more aggressive with its summer clerkship and full-time employment offers. Many firms offer so-called "exploding" offers, where the BigLaw job offer has a short expiration. For example, a student may get a summer clerkship offer with a two-day expiration.

As law students are often risk averse (which is understandable, given the over-whelming cost of law school), they dare not let an exploding offer (or really any offer) lapse and wait until public interest hiring takes place later, much less look outside of OCI.

Many law students think they should go to OCI and see what happens. Once they get a BigLaw offer, many law students are reluctant to consider alternatives for fear that the offer will disappear.

LAW STUDENTS HAVE A SHORT WINDOW TO FIGURE OUT WHERE TO START THEIR CAREER

Most law students decide where to start their legal career no later than the fall of their 3L year. In reality, many of them decide where to start their legal career well before then. That is because the majority of law students choose to start their legal career at the firm where they spend a summer during law school. For most students that is the firm that they spend their 2L summer with.

The time to decide on a 2L summer clerkship is triggered for most students by when OCI is held. Because OCI is now held earlier than in the past, there can be as little as a nine-month window from law school matriculation to a summer clerkship decision, which in many instances translates to a decision on a starting job.

And as soon as you start law school, the clock begins ticking on deciding on the path your legal career will take—which makes it even harder to avoid BigLaw. At the end of the first year (1L), few students know enough about the law to even think about becoming a lawyer, much less which of the many career paths they'd like to pursue. By the start of the third year of law school (3L), they are supposed to have everything in place to take the first steps on a career that might last forty years or longer.

By a student's 3L year, it seems that anyone who is any good has a job offer. Someone who is still interviewing in the fall of their 3L year may feel like damaged goods; they are going to prom without a date. That means law students have a very short window to educate themselves enough to make decisions about where to begin their career. Without a number of summer clerkships or much real-world knowledge, it can be very difficult to determine what is right for them.

THE BILLION-DOLLAR BigLaw PYRAMID SCHEME

BigLaw is essentially a pyramid scheme. Like any pyramid, a broad base of junior associates supports a narrowing hierarchy of senior associates and partners. To sustain this model, firms need a constant influx of new talent.

Consider the basic economics of a big law firm. Let's suppose a BigLaw firm hires 100 first-year associates, each billing $1,000 per hour for 2,000 hours annually. That would translate to $2 million in revenue from billings for each of those first-year lawyers.

Even if you assume a salary of $250K, and double that for benefits and overhead, that's only a $500K/year cost to the firm per associate. Each associate then contributes $1.5 million in gross margin to the law firm ($2M in revenue, less the $500K in expense).

That means that 100 new associates add $150 million gross revenue to the BigLaw firm's bottom line each year. If they stay on average 3 years, that is $450 million that a given incoming class of associates makes in gross margin for a BigLaw firm.

Applying this analysis to the Paul Weiss 2024 incoming class yields even bigger numbers: You have 184 associates × 2K hours × $1K/hour x 3 years, minus 184 × $500K × 3 years = **$828 million in gross margin.**

Meanwhile, BigLaw firms know that their senior associates, and ultimately, partners, will be a very small percentage of the incoming class. To them it is a very profitable numbers game. And what feeds the entire game are the large numbers of recruits that are instantly profitable for the law firm.

OCI IS ESSENTIAL TO FEEDING THIS BIGLAW PYRAMID SCHEME.

In contrast, firms that hire only a small number of lawyers per year may not find OCI worth the effort. A small boutique firm like mine may hire only two or three lawyers per year. Interviewing hundreds of candidates across dozens of different schools simply does not make economic sense.

That is why many boutiques do not participate in the OCI process, and why you will need to look beyond OCI to find a plaintiffs' lawyer career.

CHAPTER 4

The Vicious Cycle: How BigLaw Traps Students

T HIS CHAPTER IS A SHORT ASIDE *that explains why the BigLaw cycle described in the last chapter persists in law schools.*

It's also intended to help potential law students make the best possible law school choice.

There's a powerful cycle at work in how BigLaw influences law school rankings and OCI—one that reinforces itself year after year. I call it the Vicious Cycle.

Here's how it works:

When a law school places a high number of its students in BigLaw, its position in the law school rankings improves. The entities that do the rankings see BigLaw placement—and the associated salaries—as a proxy for quality. Of course, no one bothers to question what qualifies the people doing these rankings or the criteria they use in making them.

Regardless, the more students a school funnels into six-figure BigLaw jobs, the higher it climbs in the rankings. Prospective law students look at those rankings and assume they reflect educational quality, career opportunity, and ultimately, prestige. So the schools that are effective at sending students to BigLaw attract more ambitious students who are placed directly onto the BigLaw conveyor belt.

The students who survive the BigLaw jobs well enough to advance eventually become hiring partners, interviewers, and speakers. They are the ones who are sent back to OCI to be what current students see as the example for them to follow and become.

But BigLaw recruiters are not a representative sample of a law school's graduates. Instead, they are the select few BigLaw alumni who made it through the gauntlet and into BigLaw partnership. They're the ones telling students how great BigLaw is. They tell students—sometimes subtly, sometimes not—that BigLaw success is the mark of success.

Of course, they don't bother to mention the legions of their fellow lawyers who didn't make it in BigLaw (much less the obvious truth—that many of them hate their jobs).

And because students who attend OCI see only the alumni who "succeeded" at BigLaw, they too follow the same path. So, the next class sees the BigLaw graduates who "made it," hears a warped version of their "success," and blindly follows them too. And the cycle continues.

This is why so many bright, talented law students never hear a serious word about plaintiffs' law. The cycle isn't just self-reinforcing—it's exclusionary. It crowds out alternative paths, even ones that might offer greater satisfaction and long-term success.

This cycle doesn't exist to help you build a fulfilling career. It exists to keep the machine running—for the benefit of BigLaw, who profits from funneling smart, idealistic students into a rigid, high-burnout system.

The cycle isn't a conspiracy. It's just inertia.

But if you don't recognize it, you'll get swept up in it. You'll let its gravitational pull tug on your ambition and suck you in.

Alternatively, you could look beyond OCI, do your homework, and find a job that you might enjoy a heck of a lot more.

THE U.S. NEWS & WORLD REPORT, A.K.A "LIST OF SHAME"

Among the most prominent lists is the *U.S. News & World Report* 2025 law school list, which places significant weight on employment outcomes, particularly on the percentage of graduates securing BigLaw jobs. This focus incentivizes law schools to prioritize BigLaw placements to improve or maintain their rankings, which in turn pressures students to pursue OCI and BigLaw careers.

U.S. News & World Report publishes a separate ranking titled "Law Schools with the Most Graduates at BigLaw Firms," which I view as a list of shame. This ranking spotlights schools that channel a significant portion of their graduates into large law firms (defined as firms with over 250 attorneys):

Northwestern University (Pritzker)	67%
Columbia University	65%
University of Pennsylvania (Carey)	65%
University of Virginia	65%
Cornell University	63%
Duke University	59%
University of Southern California (Gould)	59%
Georgetown University	56%
Harvard University	56%
University of Chicago	56%

If I were the dean of a school funneling the majority of my graduates into BigLaw, I would be ashamed. These statistics demonstrate that these schools are not guiding their students toward varied career paths—they are simply good at keeping students on the BigLaw conveyor belt. Schools with lower BigLaw placement clearly offer a more balanced approach to career placement.

High tuition costs further exacerbate this issue. All *U.S. News* Top 10 BigLaw placement schools are private schools with an annual tuition around $80,000. In contrast, public schools that have much lower tuition, such as University of Texas, UCLA, and Georgia, see only 25 to 30 percent of their graduates enter BigLaw.

This correlation between higher tuition and higher BigLaw placement suggests that financial pressures drive students toward these jobs.

Avoiding this vicious cycle isn't easy—but if you know it's there, you can avoid being trapped inside it.

Chapter 5

The Harsh Reality of a BigLaw Career

S O WHY DOES ANY STUDENT GO TO BIGLAW? The allure of BigLaw is undeniable. It's easy to be seduced by money and alleged prestige. And a big salary to pay off a pile of student loans.

For a law student, the temptation to take the highest starting salary is very real. Most students are in a financial hole when they graduate, with student loans that averaged $220,335 in 2023.

The easiest way to pay that debt? Go work for the highest-paying firm that offers you a job ... right?

But what is life actually like as a BigLaw associate?

LIFE AS A BIGLAW ASSOCIATE IS VERY DIFFERENT THAN AS A SUMMER CLERK

Law students tell themselves they will try BigLaw out for a 1L or 2L summer clerkship. Once there, they will sip cocktails at a partner's second house, looking out over a lake, and earn more in a week than they've earned in a month. They might notice in passing that very few associates are at the social events, but they don't really think about it.

My friend interviewed for a summer clerkship at a BigLaw firm. He was walking down the hallway with people from the firm when they met a young associate coming the other way. The young associate looked him in the eye and just started silently shaking her head no, almost imperceptibly. It was as if the lawyer had been kidnapped and was unable to leave. She was giving my partner a secret signal: "Man, don't do it. Don't do it."

This is why going back to the same firm after graduation is like an episode of *Black Mirror*. That lake view is now an interior office where you are mired in the doldrums of electronic discovery and billable hours. Those hours determine your bonus because your bonus will have little to do with any results, because very little of what you do will actually matter to anyone.

More damaging to your mental health, you'll have no responsibility, and you'll learn that any promised training will always yield to the grind of the billable hour. You will barely see any of those partners who spent time recruiting you, even if you work for them.

And rather than handing you a glass of wine and ahi tartare like they did over the summer, they are handing you files. Lots and lots of files.

IF YOU WANT TO BE HAPPY, BigLaw IS ALMOST CERTAINLY THE WRONG CHOICE

Your legal career will likely last between 80,000 and 100,000 hours. How happy you are as a lawyer comes down to how much satisfaction you get from how you fill those hours. But being an associate lawyer reviewing documents for a BigLaw firm or drafting memos no one reads is demoralizing. Even if an associate makes it through the gauntlet to become a BigLaw partner, an entire career representing wrongdoers lacks meaning or reward.

At most BigLaw firms, associates are excluded from client strategy meetings. They get no meaningful responsibility and at best are invited to discovery dispute calls. They end up thinking, *This is not what I signed up for.*

Imagine that: After three years of law school, you are being paid $225,000 a year to do something a trained monkey could do (and something AI is about to take over, which we will discuss later). It is mind-numbing and soul-crushing work, especially when you are simply a cog in the larger machine and don't even understand how or what the work you do is going toward—which is how almost all junior associates operate in BigLaw.

Young lawyers assume when they start work that they will soon take the wheel, but if they are just one of a team of associates on a large case, they might never even find out where the vehicle is heading.

Big Law eats its young

Many students are led to believe that BigLaw will train them, but **the stark reality is that BigLaw has no such incentive to improve your skills.**

BigLaw is not trying to develop the long-term careers of most associates, because it is only interested in how many hours its associates can bill. BigLaw knows that the vast majority of associates will leave in three to five years, so they don't bother training the masses who won't stick around. As a result, associates rarely learn anything outside the specific tasks they are assigned.

If an incoming BigLaw class starts with one hundred associates, only ten or fifteen will be left five years later. The firm is hiring you to pump out hours for a while at the base of the pyramid. It does not want to give you experience or skills you might end up using somewhere else. It does not want to give you anything—because that costs money—and it needs only one thing from you: the billable hour that puts money in its pocket.

For the most part, as a young associate, you are completely fungible. You are the market. At least for now.

One of our younger lawyers at Reid Collins had a summer job in BigLaw where his mentor was a second-year associate (with another six levels of associates above him). The mentor would write a tiny piece of a memo that dealt with one issue. His input got plugged into something as it went up the chain—and he never saw the final memo. He had no idea of his role in the case—or even what the bigger picture was. The 1L lawyer watched his mentor work for twelve to fourteen hours a day in a suit in the summer in Houston. It was a recipe for misery.

That was when the 1L lawyer knew BigLaw was not for him. And it was not for his mentor either: The mentor lasted only another year before he quit practicing law altogether.

Many people come to the same conclusion, but do nothing about it. Two-thirds of junior and mid-level associates in BigLaw report a decline in well-being (as do 41 percent of senior associates). Eighty percent of those associates have such bad anxiety that they do not sleep well.

The vast majority of associates leave BigLaw within a few years.

But that big money is the cheese, ensuring enough young attorneys join the trap. And during an incoming class's first few years, BigLaw can identify the coveted few the firm will keep. Those who leave BigLaw go in-house or join regional or boutique firms. But once you start down the BigLaw path, it can become more difficult to pivot to a plaintiffs' law career.

BigLaw means the billable hour and defending wrongdoers

It's common knowledge that BigLaw litigation is almost all defense work. It's also well known that virtually all defense work operates on the billable hour. That means your life as a young associate is mired in filling out time sheets and meeting minimum hour requirements.

Your daily life devolves to how many billable hours you can squeeze out of every day. And it's very unlikely you will do any meaningful or interesting work. Some firms even send firmwide emails detailing each of the associates' monthly billable hours. If you're on the lower end of the report, the message is clear: get your billable hours up.

From the stories I've heard, many BigLaw recruiters talk about either pro bono work or the one cool plaintiffs' case that they handled years ago. Alternatively, they will tell you about the one trial they had in their entire career. They almost certainly do not confess that over 90 percent of what they do is defending wrongdoers. Nor do they admit that they almost never try cases.

Virtually no BigLaw firm tells you that working for BigLaw almost certainly means defense work. Very few lawyers working for BigLaw (unless they worked in government) have meaningful trial experience. In other words, *no one in BigLaw really tells it to you straight about the type of work they do, the fact that most people are unhappy, or the truth that almost no one in BigLaw actually tries cases.*

In the legal blog *Above the Law*, David Lat reported in 2023 on a presentation to new associates at the firm Paul Hastings that included a slide entitled "Non-Negotiable Expectations."

One bullet point said "You are online 24/7," and another said "'I don't know' is never an acceptable answer." The slide presented these demands as being a reflection of success: "You are in the big leagues, which is a privilege, act like it." Paul Hastings blamed the slide on an associate and claimed it did not represent the attitudes of its senior partners. Many people in the legal profession took the claim with a pinch of salt. And some probably missed it because they did not look up from their screens.

Here is something you will not learn in law school: You will likely practice in your chosen field for forty years or more. That is fifty hours a week for fifty-two weeks of the year (to be brutally honest) for forty years: a total of over 100,000 hours. If you go into BigLaw, that will seem like 300,000 hours thanks to the ongoing reliance on the billable hour, which causes many of the nation's most illustrious attorneys to count their lives in six-minute increments and dutifully record them on time sheets.

Would anyone go into BigLaw if they knew that, as an accomplished fifty-five-year old professional, they would still be parsing their life in such a way?

That is a long time to be miserable.

Imagine tracking your life in six-minute intervals

Here's an exercise. Go back to the beginning of today and log everything you did in six-minute increments. You probably showered. Hopefully brushed your teeth. Maybe stood in line for coffee. Imagine having to track your life like this.

That's the billable hour.

Almost no one in law school mentions the billable hour. They do not tell you that you must record all of your time in six-minute increments.

Worse than recording your time in tiny intervals and writing down the tasks you performed is that you generally are required to meet minimum billable hours on a monthly and annual basis. No one tells you that you will have to bill 2,000 hours per year. Nor do they tell you that it will take over sixty hours per week to bill that much time.

When it comes to minimum hours, you probably did the sums in your head as a law student and decided, "OK, 2,000 hours in a year doesn't sound too bad. Take off two weeks' holiday, divide the total by fifty, and that's forty hours a week."

If you are working, you know that billable hours and working hours are not the same thing. It takes far longer than sixty minutes to be able to bill a whole hour, because you have to get a bite to eat; you have to go to recruiting functions or staff meetings; you meet people in the corridor and chat; or you go grab a coffee.

Yale Law School explains this to students in a presentation with two scenarios in which an associate has to bill 1,800 hours and 2,200 hours, respectively. Allowing for breaks for coffee or lunch, reading legal updates, dealing with general correspondence, and attending meetings and conferences, an associate billing 1,832 hours would need to work 2,420 hours, while an associate billing 2,200 hours would need to work 3,058 hours.

In a fifty-week year—although most junior associates effectively work fifty-two weeks a year—that is at least seventeen hours of unbilled hours per week on top of your billed hours.

This means a forty-hour workweek is actually a fifty-seven-hour workweek, which means over eight hours a day *every day of the week.*

The Yale report reminds law students, "Keep in mind that these schedules do not account for personal calls at work, training/observing, talking with coworkers, a longer lunch (to exercise or shop perhaps), a family funeral, pro bono work (if not treated as billable hours), serving on a bar committee, writing an article for the bar journal, or interviewing an applicant."

What about just living your life? I think you might want some time for that, right?

Yale advises students to question firms at OCI about their policy on billable hours (our policy at Reid Collins is that we don't even have time sheets). But yes, if you're going to a firm that primarily bills by the hour, you need to know its billing policies.

For example, does the firm have minimum hours, does training and pro bono count toward those hours, etc.?

This all means that a young associate at BigLaw will end up working most of every weekend, because finding the hours during the week is hard. It means spending long hours in the office. You can try to make your Friday nights or Saturday mornings sacred, but it might not make any difference. You may enjoy close friendships with your colleagues because you are all in the same boat and you will be sharing lots of takeout. You might even see romantic relationships evolve, because the other associates are the only people you ever see.

You can take comfort from the fact that you are all in it together . . . but really you are all commiserating because you are under siege together.

It's a very common experience for a young associate to find that every time they have an independent idea, their boss tells them, "We're not doing that. Just do what I told you to do and bill your hours."

It comes as a shock to many new law graduates that they have to fill out time sheets every day or every week. It's dehumanizing to detail your life in increments of one-tenth of an hour, but this is going to measure out your whole career: 0.3 phone call with John, 0.1 reading email from Susie, and so on.

To make things worse, at the end of the week it is not unusual to think, *I only have thirty-three hours, I need forty.* Exhausted associates might be tempted to think, *Well, that 0.3 call was really 0.5. And the brief that I wrote for 1.2, let's make that 1.5.* Their time expands to meet their required hours. The time sheet becomes fiction. And the whole exercise is demoralizing (not to mention, possibly fraudulent).

No matter how diligent anyone is, billing is an imprecise science that relies on an individual's ethics. Billable hours are subjective. A billable hour for one lawyer will be different from a billable hour for another. The dividing line between what is billable and what is not is unclear. You will always be interrupted, and some of those interruptions will slip through.

In fact, you're perversely incentivized to let things slip through. If you are not comfortable with overbilling (I was not), you will end up being in the office a lot of weekends (I was).

You might think, *My personal ethics are very clear. I'll just bill the hours I work.* Most people feel like that, but consider what I call the airplane question. If you have to fly for four hours to meet a client or attend a hearing but you spend the flight working for another client, can you bill the first client for your travel time while you also bill the second for your work? You'd double your hours—and neither client would have any grounds to complain.

Some law firms hold seminars on billing "efficiency" for associates, but their seminars are not about being time efficient and saving clients money; they are aimed at making associates more efficient at recording *all of their time*. Other firms circulate memos telling associates how to "optimize" their billing: But again, optimizing does not mean saving clients money. It is a euphemism for managing your time sheets so not a moment is unaccounted for. It effectively encourages overbilling.

Some firms look the other way, even when overbilling is obvious. Why? Overbilling makes the law firm money and the engagement partner reviewing the bills has a personal economic incentive to allow it. Including your padded bills makes him more money. It is no surprise that many young lawyers end up massaging their hours.

About thirty years ago I shared a secretary with a lawyer whose "creative billing" meant he claimed to have worked twenty-five hours in a twenty-four-hour day. The secretary told him, "The system won't take it." He told her, "Just dump the extra hour into the next day."

The truth is that BigLaw cares far more if you bill 2,375 billable hours a year than if you bill 1,900 hours and come up with a great idea to win a case. Although the lack of responsibility is demoralizing, for many young associates, $4,000 a week is a hell of a sweetener, so a lot of people take it and suffer through the work.

But it is like putting sugar on horseshit. The cash draws you in, like an addict. You pay off more of your student loan, but then buy a house, a new BMW, expensive clothes, etc. Or you live in a high-cost area where most of your money goes to accommodation, food, and taxes. Either way, you get more and more dependent on the money.

It is what's called the golden handcuffs. You are trapped in such comfort that you might not even realize that you're stuck. Until you try to walk away.

Making partner likely won't get you what you want

Some law students believe there is only one ambition worth having: making partner in a BigLaw firm. Being a partner has long been seen as the pinnacle of a legal career. But it is not the right goal for everyone, and for some people, it can be positively damaging.

Law firms are getting bigger—and the trend is accelerating.

As of 2024, Baker McKenzie, one of the largest US-based firms, employed over 4,700 lawyers worldwide. In a significant development, KPMG, one of the Big Four accounting firms, received approval from the Arizona Supreme Court in early 2025 to launch KPMG Law US, making it the first of the Big Four to offer legal services in the United States. This move is part of Arizona's Alternative Business

Structure (ABS) program, which allows nonlawyers to have economic interests in law firms—a model already prevalent in Europe. As accounting giants expand into legal services, BigLaw firms are poised to grow even bigger.

But while the size of firms continues to grow, the number of equity partners has stalled. In the distant past, you served your time, you climbed the ladder, and you hoped to be the one or two of your first-year class to make equity partner. That is not how it works anymore. In fact, most firms have two tiers of partners— equity and non-equity. A non-equity partner is essentially an employee with the title of partner. It is only equity partners that own part of a firm, and they are becoming increasingly rare.

Today, you frankly have more of a chance of being eaten by a shark than making equity partner at many firms.

The megafirms are pyramids with lots of people at the bottom, very little room at the top, and very few ladders. Reaching the peak is forbiddingly hard. If you are a young associate at a thousand-lawyer firm and you are not in the main office or you are not working for one of the partners on the executive committee, you are nobody. Even if you have a genius idea, like an insight that wins a case, it is hard to be recognized.

At OCI, every candidate asks how long the "partnership" pathway takes. And virtually every BigLaw firm gives you a rehearsed answer: "Oh, it's about ten years." Of course, without knowing that there is a difference between equity and non-equity, how do you even interpret the answer?

Not many students follow up with the real question: "What percentage of your entering class typically make *equity* partner?" Or the other important question: "How many lateral equity partners (lawyers hired from other firms) do you have?"

In some firms, the percentage of associates who go on to make equity partner might be as low as 1 to 3 percent.

Imagine this, because it happens all time:

Your work as an associate lawyer is not satisfying, but you churn through it because you tell yourself you will make partner one day. You give your firm its 2,200 hours a year. You go to all the events and check all the boxes. You defend causes you dislike: financially greedy bad actors, tobacco, opioids, polluters, and other wrongdoers. You struggle to balance your family life with work. Your mental and physical health suffer.

And then, in year eight, your firm brings in a lateral partner more senior than you, blocking your rise in the partner pyramid. And in year ten, your firm makes you a partner, but you realize that it's just a title and that you are a non-equity, "service" partner with no ownership in the firm.

In the past, white-shoe law firms relied solely on their in-house partnership path, the same way baseball teams used to hire only farm prospects. In other words, law firm partnerships used to be populated exclusively by associates who rose through the ranks. But just like baseball introduced free agency so players could move around, now even the best firms hire lateral partners. On the flip side, in the past virtually no one ever left a white-shoe firm to practice law elsewhere, but that's also more common now.

BigLaw is the Past, not the Future

Let's get this straight: BigLaw is not the future of law. It's the past. And AI is about to make that painfully obvious.

For the better part of a century, BigLaw grew by scale. Firms merged to offer clients full-service coverage—corporate, tax, litigation, employment—under one roof. The idea was simple: never let a client walk out the door. At bottom the question was "How do we maximize the revenue from a client that has multiple legal needs?"

If I'm the BigLaw litigation partner and my client needs a transactional lawyer, I walk them down the hall and refer them to my transactional partner—even if he's mediocre. I'll still sell my partner to the client and call him "brilliant," because I get origination credit for keeping the work in-house.

It works if everyone plays ball. Spoiler alert: They don't. There are turf wars in every law firm.

I know a BigLaw lawyer who landed a client. The client needed corporate transactional work and so he referred the client to a partner in the corporate department. His partner took the matter—then quietly opened her own billing file and stole the origination credit. This kind of thing happens all the time. Turf wars. Backstabbing. Internal politics disguised as collaboration.

AI IS COMING FOR THE BILLABLE HOUR

And now the entire BigLaw model is about to break. AI is coming for the billable hour—and that hour is the lifeblood of BigLaw. When AI can generate a memo in thirty seconds, review thousands of documents in a minute, or draft a motion in real time, things are going to change. Perhaps a single lawyer, using AI, can produce a final product in a few hours. No client is going to pay $900 to $2,500 per hour for a team of lawyers to do the same work that a single lawyer can accomplish with AI help.

I believe that the efficiencies created by AI will disrupt BigLaw, ending its use of the billable hour. When that happens there will be far fewer lawyers needed and the pyramid scheme will no longer work.

BIGLAW WILL TRANSFORM FROM A PYRAMID TO A WINE BOTTLE.

In the past, each part of the country had a handful of top firms filled with prestigious partners. Aggregation has left very few regional firms, creating a landscape of supposed haves (BigLaw), and have-nots (everyone else).

By most metrics there are only around twenty BigLaw firms in the US that "matter." When I say matter, I mean in terms of getting the biggest cases on a regular basis, having the biggest impact . . . and making the most money. The rest are aggregating as fast as possible for survival (and are often dependent on litigation finance or borrowed money).

The chasm between the top twenty or so firms and the rest is enormous. The wealth divide between firms is glaringly obvious to anyone paying attention.

How much is your life worth?

If you choose BigLaw knowing all of this, that's your choice, but at least be very clear about this to yourself. You will potentially make money, but you will sell your life to do it. No one in law school tells you this stark reality.

You will certainly make a great salary at BigLaw, but it will come at a cost. First, you will gain little or no experience. Worse, you will become accustomed to the high salary and it will make moving to a job that will gain you experience more difficult.

There is a larger price to this as well from a mental health perspective. In 2024, the divorce rate for lawyers and judges in the United States was 28 percent, higher than the national average (the average statistics are given in the form of 16.9 divorces per 1,000 married women).

A 2020 article by Harrison Barnes reasoned that the *bigger* the firm a lawyer works in, the *higher* the divorce rate—particularly among litigators. Barnes recalled working at a large litigation firm where every single attorney had been divorced.

Something most young lawyers don't realize: Happiness is not as much what you get paid from the job, it is more the reward and meaning you get from the work you do on the job.

Did your efforts make a real impact on someone?

No one brags to their grandkids that they saved Goldman Sachs $2 billion in a bond sale. No one's obituary says they saved Bank of America billions of dollars it should have paid for the harm it caused in connection with the 2008 financial crisis.

Junior associates work extremely hard, and in financial terms, they are rewarded well. They can pay their student debt, buy a nice car, live in a nice house or apartment, eat expensive meals, and pay for cool trips.

But then they start living up to their means, so they end up with a house to support, private schools, expensive hobbies, the whole American dream. Their work makes them miserable but there is no way out. That's the trade-off they chose when they decided to measure their life in six-minute increments.

What does that mean for you as a junior associate? It means that, in the eyes of BigLaw, *your commodity is your time, not your effectiveness.*

Let's do the basic math for you: Even at $225,000 a year, you are selling your life at between $75 and $100 an hour, depending on usage rate. Meanwhile, the law firm is charging $1,000 per hour or more for your time.

You're selling your life at a 90 percent discount . . . for what?

How hard will you work at the funeral?

Even if young lawyers understand all of the problems with BigLaw, the allure of making partner is still attractive to some. But not only is partnership hard to obtain, it is not what you think it is once you get it. Take this story:

Gabe MacConaill was a forty-two-year old bankruptcy lawyer at Sidley Austin who took his own life in 2018. His wife wrote an article entitled "'BigLaw Killed My Husband': An Open Letter from a Sidley Partner's Widow." MacConaill had reached the pinnacle in BigLaw: He was a young equity partner. Yet it was not enough.

Or this story. When Peter Zimmerman, a senior partner at Wilson Sonsini, died in 2020, his wife, Eilene, wrote a book about his two addictions: to work, and to the drugs that eventually killed him. Even as his senior colleagues were giving the eulogies at Zimmerman's funeral, she wrote, the church was full of young associates writing emails on their phones.

If that's not fucked up, what is?

The consequences of your career choice can be deadly.

CHAPTER 6:

Don't Sleepwalk into the
Wrong Career

THERE ARE SO MANY THINGS TO CONSIDER when choosing your legal career, yet law students often skip over the basics. If you start to think about the end of your career and looking back over decades of law practice—what will you be proud of? What will matter to you about the work that you've done?

Of course, any legal career worth being proud of requires something meaningful and rewarding. And there are many studies suggesting that the lawyers who make less money but have greater purpose (e.g., public defenders and public interest lawyers) are happier than lawyers who make more money (i.e., BigLaw). This is not a question of moral superiority. It's about personal fulfillment. It's about knowing that your life's work meant something. These are questions you'll need to answer for yourself.

I met a law student recently who told me, "I think I want to be a tax lawyer." I asked him, "Why on earth would you want to do that?" He said, "Well, I was an accountant so I've had some exposure to taxation and I like it."

I told him, "I was an accountant before I went into law, and I love numbers, but I still think I'd hate tax law. Do you realize you'll only interact with other tax lawyers or financial professionals on the most esoteric and arcane tax issues? And when you look back, at best, you will be able to say, 'I solved complex tax problems and I ultimately helped people avoid paying taxes for the entirety of my career.' Do you think you could be passionate about that? Do you think you could find meaning in a career as a tax lawyer? Would you look back on your career with a sense of pride and accomplishment?"

He said, "No, I doubt I would ever be passionate about tax law. And I doubt there would be much meaning either." I told him, "Keep looking." The student concluded, "I've never thought about it like that."

But that is exactly how *every* law student should think about it. A career spent on meaningful and rewarding work will provide a great deal of happiness. Consequently, it is critically important to think about what a specific career would lead to. Ask yourself: Would I find true meaning in a career focused on [x or y]?

Here are some questions you should consider:

1. What sort of work do you want to do?
2. Where do you want to live?
3. Who do you want to spend your time with?
4. What area of the law is most exciting to you?
5. Are you interested in the actual work you'd do in that area?
6. Would you be able to make a positive difference in people's lives?
7. Do you think you'll be able to look back on a career and have a real sense of accomplishment?

If you fail to educate yourself about alternative career paths in the law, you run the risk of sleepwalking into something you will not enjoy, just like the tax lawyer example. And to be quite frank, that is the single most likely reason that the majority of lawyers are unhappy—they did not take the time to think through what a meaningful career path would be for them.

At least the wannabe tax lawyer had thought enough to have a preference. Many young lawyers do not get that far. Many young lawyers simply think, *I need to make $225,000 in starting salary and I will figure out the rest.* If you do not make your own plan, you will be following someone else's . . . and it is likely to lead you toward BigLaw.

Let me tell you about two young lawyers named Abby and Julia.

ABBY GOT SUCKED INTO BigLaw AND IT ENDED HER CAREER

When Abby arrived at law school, she planned on practicing public interest law because she wanted to help people. As she was a talented writer, her teachers advised her to go to law school before going on to run a nonprofit. She thought that she might like to be an environmental lawyer.

At law school, Abby explained her goals to her career development advisors, who pressed her to go to OCI and consider a BigLaw career. "If you do it for a few years," they told her, "you'll be set up for life."

At OCI, Abby got sucked in by BigLaw. She found a BigLaw job doing environmental law. She was sucked in by the apparent prestige, the allure of training, and of course the huge starting salary. So, she signed up for BigLaw as a detour on her way to public interest with the enticement of training and good pay.

What she didn't fully realize was that BigLaw meant hourly fee, defense work. She soon found herself defending large corporations accused of environmental wrongdoing.

In other words, *she was defending the very people she went to law school to prosecute.*

Even worse for Abby, she was given no responsibility and zero autonomy. Abby spent the next few years doing menial chores with no control over her time and little useful training. She got burned out from working over 2,000 hours a year. The money was great, but it couldn't make up for menial work, minimal responsibility, lack of training, and being shut out from the bigger picture.

In the end, Abby did not just quit her job. She quit the legal profession altogether.

She became a writer, an artist—and a statistic. She never even went into the public interest work she originally desired, because she was so burned out on being a lawyer.

She is among the one in five associates who leave the practice of law every year.

Joining BigLaw to prepare for public service is like joining the Mafia to prepare to be a social worker.

It didn't work for Abby and it won't work for you.

Julia avoided BigLaw and loves her career as a plaintiffs' lawyer

Let me tell you about Julia. She arrived at Stanford Law School knowing she wanted to be a plaintiffs' lawyer thanks to a random work placement.

As a college sophomore, Julia was offered a chance to shadow a college alum, and she spent a week at a two-attorney, plaintiff-side employment firm in New York. The attorneys explained that they represented people in cases against their employers for various forms of discrimination, including race, sex, and disability.

They told Julia about a client who worked at a care home. The woman had been diagnosed with cancer, and had to regularly receive chemotherapy treatments during work hours. Rather than be compassionate and understanding, her asshole employers fired her because her lifesaving treatments interfered with their priorities.

Julia thought, *What the fuck? They need to pay for what they did. You can't act like such a callous asshole without consequences.*

The plaintiffs' lawyers handed Julia a binder and said, "We have a motion where the defense wants to image our client's entire phone as part of discovery. That would require an image of all contents in our client's phone, including all of her personal data. Can you figure out a way to fight this?"

Even though she had not even attended law school yet, Julia recalled reading about a case on privacy, so the partners encouraged her to try to find it. Even though she was not a lawyer, Julia found the case, which supported the argument they were looking for.

Julia highlighted the portions of the opinion she thought could support an argument that the client was not obligated to turn over her phone. The partners ended up using Julia's case and her privacy argument to fight the discovery issue. Eventually, the court sided with them on the discovery issue and soon thereafter they settled the case.

Even though she was not a lawyer, by using the law, Julia was able to make a difference. After only a week working on that small case, Julia's relatively modest contribution to it sold her on becoming a plaintiffs' lawyer. She later returned to that law firm as a paralegal throughout college.

Right before her senior year, Julia was able to attend the first few days of a trial in a race discrimination employment case in St. Louis, Missouri. The city is diverse, but segregated. The lawyers needed to get people to talk about race in jury selection because race is obviously relevant in a race discrimination case.

Again, Julia as a nonlawyer read up about bias and race, then helped write the voir dire questions for jury selection. The questions started a conversation among a large panel of over one hundred potential jurors, who were soon having a discussion among themselves, moderated by the attorney.

During opening statements, Julia sat at counsel table like a real lawyer. She also watched the client give her testimony. The client eventually won an $8.5 million verdict, which was the largest race discrimination employment verdict in Missouri history.

As a nonlawyer, sitting in and participating in her first trial, Julia was fascinated by it all. She was hooked on plaintiffs' law, but not hooked on discrimination work. She sampled her first taste of plaintiffs' law and liked it, but wanted to try other types of plaintiffs' law.

When Julia arrived at Stanford Law School she was one of the rare students who knew that she wanted to be a plaintiffs' lawyer; she just didn't know what kind of plaintiffs' lawyer she wanted to be.

Julia did a few things during law school that enabled her to reach her goal of being a plaintiffs' lawyer. First, she avoided OCI like the plague. On her own, Julia realized much of what I've said about OCI in this book. Second, Julia and some of her fellow classmates revived the Stanford chapter of the Plaintiffs' Law Association.

But most importantly, Julia sampled a number of law firms during her 1L and 2L summers. One of those firms was my firm. Julia researched nationally prominent plaintiffs' firms and read up about them. Then she sent a thoughtful, targeted email to me inquiring about a summer clerkship. I could not help but be impressed by Julia's targeted outreach. Here was a law student who had avoided OCI and found my firm all on her own. That by itself was impressive.

When I spoke with Julia, I was even more impressed. She already knew that she did not want to work for BigLaw, she knew that she wanted to be a plaintiffs' lawyer, and she wanted to sample other types of plaintiffs' law. She was intrigued by my firm's complex financial litigation practice and wanted to try it as a summer clerk.

Julia eventually came to work for my firm during her 2L summer. She was equally impressive on the job. Today, she is an associate at my firm, and she loves her job.

Meanwhile, Abby had a faceless, anonymous experience in BigLaw and she ended up quitting law altogether.

Two promising law students. Two young lawyers with great potential. Two lawyers I would likely have been happy to hire. But only one lawyer who found a path that enabled her to love the law and the work she does.

PART 2:

THE CASE FOR A CAREER IN PLAINTIFFS' LAW

CHAPTER 7:

Plaintiffs' Lawyers Are Legal Heroes

WHO INSPIRED YOU TO BECOME A LAWYER? I say *who*, not *what*, because it is impossible to grow up in America without being surrounded by lawyers in movies, TV, or books.

Who did you want to be? Atticus Finch, in his seersucker suit, who braves the wrath of the whole town to defend unjustly accused Tom Robinson in *To Kill a Mockingbird*?

Elle Woods, who surprises everyone and wins on her own terms in *Legally Blonde*? Harvey Specter from *Suits*, with all of his swagger?

Or maybe Mickey Haller, running his law practice from the back seat of his Lincoln in the Michael Connelly book *The Lincoln Lawyer*?

Ally McBeal? Ben Matlock? Perry Mason? The list goes on . . . but all of them fought bullies.

Whoever inspired you, I can guarantee one thing: It was *not* someone who played a BigLaw attorney.

Most fictional legal heroes are either plaintiffs' lawyers or criminal defense attorneys.

What do they all have in common? They fight bullies.

And this is one of the rare times Hollywood gets it right. Because in real life too, no one cheers for the bully.

This holds true in life as well:

The majority of real legal heroes are plaintiffs' attorneys.

The only difference between Hollywood and the real world here is that you probably haven't heard of many of their names—though you almost certainly know the impact of the work they've done.

There are literally countless examples of all the societal changes brought about by plaintiffs' lawyers. Look at some of the greatest advances in public safety and justice in the last century, and in many instances you will find plaintiffs' lawyers at the heart of them.

Plaintiffs' lawyers made cars much safer: The Ford Pinto case

In the 1970s, Ford rolled out the Pinto—a cheap, fuel-efficient car. It also came with a hidden time bomb. The Pinto's fuel tank was mounted in a deadly spot. Nearby bolts and sharp edges turned crashes into infernos.

Ford knew it. Their own crash tests showed the Pinto exploded again and again. Before it ever sold a single Pinto, Ford conducted internal tests, which showed that the fuel tank ruptured in nearly every rear-end collision. The tests showed that this problem would occur even at speeds *as low as 20 mph.*

Engineers proposed simple, cheap fixes:

- A rubber membrane inside the tank
- A plastic baffle outside
- A metal shield over the axle

The cost? *Eleven dollars per car.*

But Ford's executives ran the numbers another way.

The critical piece of evidence that the plaintiffs' lawyers used in the Pinto case was a cost-benefit analysis that Ford had submitted to the National Highway Traffic Safety Administration ("NHTSA").

In the memo, Ford coldly calculated the "cost" of human life:

- **$200,000** for a death
- **$67,000** for an injury
- **$700** for property damage

Then they crunched the numbers:

- **$49 million** in estimated payouts to victims
- **$137 million** to fix the design

The choice was obvious to them. The cost to fix the problem was greater than the expected consequences of sending the Pinto to market with its deadly flaws.

As a result, *Ford deliberately chose not to fix the problem, and people were killed and injured.*

Mark Robinson and Arthur Hews represented the plaintiffs in *Grimshaw v. Ford Motor Company,* which became one of the most significant product liability cases in US history. The case was based on the allegation that Ford Motor Company sold a car that it knew had a dangerous and defective fuel system. The plaintiffs' lawyers' work exposed Ford's criminal negligence and led to significant changes in auto safety standards.

Using Ford's own memo, the plaintiffs' lawyers argued that Ford had chosen not to fix the problem that it knew existed because it would have cost more to fix the problem than to await litigation and pay the dead and injured. They synthesized this argument by arguing that Ford should be held accountable for choosing profits over human lives.

After years of litigation, which Ford lost, they had to recall 1.5 million Pintos and the model was taken off the market. And, although it was later acquitted, Ford Motor Company was indicted and charged criminally. This was the first time that a US corporation was ever indicted.

Obviously, Ford had seriously miscalculated the cost of sending a deadly product to market. But had it not been for the plaintiffs' lawyers, Ford would not have been forced to recall the product, and many more injuries and deaths would've occurred.

Because of plaintiffs' lawyers, auto companies and other product manufacturers learned the costly lesson that they could not ignore safety without a fight.

PLAINTIFFS' LAWYERS—NOT THE GOVERNMENT—TOOK DOWN BIG TOBACCO

In the 1980s, the horrendous consequences of smoking were becoming too big to ignore. Big Tobacco had dodged liability for decades, hiding behind an army of defense lawyers, junk science, and political influence. But in 1998 they were finally made to pay—and only because of the efforts of some now famous (and rich) plaintiffs' lawyers.

A coalition of state attorneys general and private plaintiffs' lawyers joined forces and brought cases across the country. Keep in mind, no one had ever won a case against a tobacco company in the decades since plaintiffs' lawyers began trying to make them pay for what they were doing.

After years of litigation, the tobacco lawyers reached a gargantuan $200 billion settlement to cover smoking-related health care costs. The settlement also imposed significant restrictions on tobacco advertising, which in turn have led to consistent declines in smoking.

The Texas litigation is the one I know the most about. In the landmark Texas tobacco settlement, five plaintiffs' lawyers collectively secured a $3.3 billion fee for their work negotiating a historic $17.6 billion settlement with major tobacco companies in 1998 for the State of Texas medical programs.

These lawyers were:

- John Eddie Williams
- Walter Umphrey
- Harold Nix
- Wayne Reaud
- John O'Quinn

These lawyers, often referred to as the "Big Five," were contracted by Texas Attorney General Dan Morales to represent the state in its lawsuit against the tobacco industry. Most Texas lawyers old enough to remember the tobacco settlement know all of these names. Each of these lawyers got rich because they were willing to take the risk and as a result were able to reap the massive reward.

As with many cases, a whistleblower played a critical role in exposing the many lies that the tobacco industry had been hiding behind. The whistleblower part of the story was told in the Al Pacino and Russell Crowe movie *The Insider*, which realistically captured the drama of a whistleblower risking everything to expose Big Tobacco's deadly secrets.

The tobacco cases proved what happens when plaintiffs' lawyers take action—even against the biggest, richest bullies in the world.

Plaintiffs' lawyers ended the sale of asbestos

Attorneys like Fred Baron, Ron Motley, and Paul Hanly Jr. were instrumental in uncovering the asbestos industry's cover-up of the dangers of asbestos exposure.

For decades, the asbestos industry knew their product was deadly. Yet they hid this evidence. The asbestos manufacturers and their army of defense lawyers paid hundreds of confidential settlements through the workers' compensation system to keep their deadly secret. They knew that asbestos was killing people, but like Ford, they decided that the cost of fixing the problem outweighed the problem. Thanks to plaintiffs' lawyers, they too would be proven wrong.

Like early waves of tobacco litigation, the early efforts to hold asbestos manufacturers accountable also failed. It took until the 1970s for plaintiffs' lawyers to change things.

In the famous case of *Borel v. Fibreboard Paper Products*, the estate of Clarence Borel won the first big lawsuit against an asbestos manufacturer. By the 1980s and 1990s, over 700,000 claims were brought against over 8,000 companies. This tsunami of litigation led to the creation of over sixty trusts, funded with tens of billions of dollars to pay asbestos victims' claims.

Interestingly, although the EPA tried to ban asbestos, its attempts were overturned. As a result, asbestos sales were never fully banned by the US government.

In other words, the government could not stop manufacturers from continuing their deadly practices—it was only plaintiffs' lawyers' efforts that ended the sale and manufacture of asbestos.

Plaintiffs' lawyers save the environment

Countless plaintiffs' lawyers have played a critical role in protecting our environment and winning cases against asshole corporations that have found it more profitable to pollute than operate their business safely.

Recently, there have been a number of prominent environmental cases, such as the Flint, Michigan case in which plaintiffs' lawyers proved that the local government knew that its public water supply was contaminated with lead.

Two examples of cool environmental cases became popular movies.

Jan Schlichtmann gained national attention for his role in a major environmental case portrayed in the book and film called *A Civil Action*. Schlichtmann represented several families in Woburn, Massachusetts, who alleged that their children's leukemia was caused by contamination of the town's groundwater supply. The defendants, including major companies like W.R. Grace & Co. and Beatrice Foods, were found liable for improperly disposing of toxic chemicals that ultimately migrated into municipal wells. Of course, Schlichtmann is the hero in the movie.

In another high-profile environmental case, Erin Brockovich (though not an attorney herself) played a critical role in uncovering widespread groundwater contamination in Hinkley, California. Residents of Hinkley had been exposed to toxic chemicals that PG&E had improperly discharged into the environment over several decades. Brockovich's investigation, including door-to-door community outreach and collection of medical evidence, helped build the foundation for the mass tort action.

The Hinkley litigation culminated in 1996 with a $333 million settlement—the largest of its kind at the time—providing compensation to hundreds of victims. Brockovich's work demonstrated the impact that plaintiffs' lawyers can have in protecting public health and environmental safety.

The cumulative deterrent effect of the efforts of these and other environmental plaintiffs' lawyers have led to a safer world for all of us.

How plaintiffs' law saved people from Smithfield Foods

Smithfield Foods was operating huge hog houses in North Carolina that each held 10,000 hogs. Think about it—that's a lot of hogs.

Unfortunately, they built all of these hog houses right next to a residential area. But because the people in the neighboring residential area were relatively uneducated and poor, Smithfield didn't care very much about them.

All the hog waste from the shitload of hogs was washed into an area the size of a football field. When the field was literally full of shit, Smithfield Foods didn't dispose of it properly because that would have cost too much, so they just sprayed it into the air, because that was the cheapest and most profitable option for their business.

They were literally shitting on their poor neighbors.

These neighbors were 550 black Americans who'd inherited the land they lived on from their enslaved great-grandparents. They got tired of taking this shit from Smithfield Foods, and hired Lisa Blue, a well-known environmental and toxic tort lawyer, to help them make Smithfield Foods pay for all of this crap.

When Lisa tested her clients' homes, she found hog shit in their kitchens, in their refrigerators, even on the bread in the baskets on their tables. It was quite literally disgusting.

In 2013, Lisa sued Smithfield Foods in Raleigh, North Carolina, seeking hundreds of millions of dollars. Rather than admit their responsibility, Smithfield Foods lobbied the North Carolina government to pass a law that would give the hog industry immunity. Lisa had to spend hundreds of thousands of dollars hiring a lobbyist to fight the law, and she ultimately succeeded in blocking it.

In 2019, after six years of fighting the case, Smithfield Foods finally settled for many hundreds of millions of dollars. More importantly, Smithfield Foods was forced to stop spraying shit on their neighbors.

Lisa's case is a great example of how plaintiffs' law can bring together a combination of idealism, social justice, and good business sense. Sure, Lisa made a handsome fee, but she earned it. And she really accomplished something for her clients.

By the way, because of what she saw in the Smithfield Foods case, Lisa has never eaten meat since.

In my opinion, Lisa is a real legal hero.

PLAINTIFFS' LAWYERS—NOT THE GOVERNMENT—ENDED THE OPIOID CRISIS

The story of the opioid crisis is shocking. The corporations that sold massive quantities of opioids literally made billions of dollars. They also killed over *one million Americans.*

To me, the work that plaintiffs' lawyers did to end the opioid crisis is a sterling example of the critical role plaintiffs' lawyers can play in addressing public health disasters.

One of the lawyers who played a prominent role in taking down the opioid manufacturers was my good friend Brad Beckworth, who is a partner at the firm Nix Patterson.

In 2015, Brad took one of his clients, a famous professional athlete, to a rehab facility. Over 80 percent of the patients in that facility were there because they were addicted to opioids. Many started on the path to addiction with a prescription pill that they casually took for pain.

Brad soon realized that there were literally thousands and thousands of stories like his client's story. Brad discussed the opioid epidemic with his mentor Reggie Whitten, an Oklahoma lawyer whose son died in a motorcycle accident after driving while under the influence of opioids. Whitten had spent a decade educating high school and college athletes around the country on opioid addiction since the death of his son.

Whitten recommended that Brad read *Dreamland* by *LA Times* writer Sam Quinones. The book describes how the OxyContin crisis started in Appalachia and Ohio. Whitten told Brad, "I've always thought the problem was driven by the drug manufacturers. If this book makes sense, call me."

A couple of days later, Brad called Whitten and said, "It makes sense. This is tobacco all over again. It's something that you and I have been brought together to do."

The two lawyers decided to take on the opioid industry. They approached Mike Hunter, then attorney general of Oklahoma, and told him all about the opioid epidemic and the role that big corporations had played in it. They further explained that Oklahoma had some of the worst opioid problems in the country.

Soon thereafter Hunter hired Brad to file Oklahoma's lawsuit against the opioid industry. He was committed to be the first opioid case to go to trial in the country. This would be no small task.

As the trial approached, Brad and his team worked twenty hours a day. Although there were lawsuits in every state, Brad's Oklahoma case was the first to go to trial. As a result, the drug manufacturers focused all of their efforts on the Oklahoma case. Brad faced a team of over one hundred lawyers.

Just before the trial, Brad settled with Purdue Pharma for $270 million. The Purdue settlement drove Purdue into bankruptcy and exposed the Sackler family that owned it to billions of dollars in liability.

The next settlement was against the Israeli company Teva for $85 million.

That left one company to go to trial: Johnson & Johnson. Everyone had heard about their baby powder, but virtually no one knew about their role in the opioid crisis. Johnson & Johnson had created a mutant, more potent poppy to produce oxyco-done, the active ingredient in opioids. In order to stay under the radar, Johnson & Johnson used a manufacturing facility in Tasmania, which became the world's number one supplier of oxycodone.

During the case, Brad showed a picture of the Tasmanian poppy fields. The photo was taken by a doctor named Andrew Kolodny, who discovered Johnson & Johnson's facility in Tasmania. Brad and his team used Kolodny as one of their primary expert witnesses.

Kolodny worked with Brad for two years. He told them, "The story no one knows is that Johnson & Johnson is the kingpin of the opioid crisis. That's the story that people need to hear. The public and law enforcement need to understand that this problem is being driven by companies that make baby shampoo and Q-tips but are really drug dealers."

Johnson & Johnson tried to delay the trial, but when that did not work, they hired a talented army of defense lawyers and got ready. The trial was televised live on six continents. In the two hours after Brad's opening statement, Johnson & Johnson's market capitalization fell by $25 billion. For the first time, people heard about Johnson & Johnson's unknown role in the opioid crisis.

The trial took two weeks, and the plaintiffs won a $572 million verdict. Brad's team lost the Johnson & Johnson verdict on appeal on a legal issue. Although Johnson & Johnson escaped liability in Oklahoma, they nonetheless entered into a $5 billion global settlement. Brad's other client, the State of Washington, recovered $149.5 million of that settlement from Johnson & Johnson.

Ultimately, in spite of the appellate loss in the Johnson & Johnson case, Oklahoma recovered over $1 billion from all of the opioid-related litigation that it pursued.

Brad's twenty-person law firm was about $14 million in the hole by the time of the trial. For the better part of two years they had not been able to bring in any revenue because this was all they were working on. But they took the risk and they earned a massive contingency fee.

But most importantly, they took down an industry and made them pay for what they did. The opioid example—like the tobacco example and many others before it—demonstrates the power that plaintiffs' lawyers have to drive major social change.

There are countless legal heroes

For virtually every public health and safety victory, there's a plaintiffs' lawyer (or a team of them) who fought that battle. Seat belt laws, warning labels on cigarettes, safer medical procedures—plaintiffs' litigation played a critical role in all of these.

And the list goes on. There are literally *thousands of examples* of the same sorts of cases, where plaintiffs' lawyers have made a difference, and made the world better.

The majority of real-life legal "heroes"—the ones who actually protect people and change society—have been plaintiffs' lawyers.

Think about it—there are no movies or books in which a BigLaw partner is the hero.

CHAPTER 8

Plaintiffs' Lawyers Choose Their Clients and Cases

I N ALL OF MY CASES, I REQUIRE that the equities favor my client or I refuse the case. What I mean by "equities" is which side is in the "right" and which side is in the "wrong."

In order to decide if the equities support taking a case, I focus not only on the equities themselves, but also on the nature and extent of the plaintiff's harm and the level of the defendant's wrongdoing and how egregious it is.

In effect, I ask which side, the plaintiff or defendant, do I prefer to be on? And, relatedly, how compelled would I be to award damages to the plaintiff if I were the judge or jury?

I ask myself two questions:

1. "Is the plaintiff's case sympathetic?" and
2. "Does the defendant need to pay for what they have done?"

Ideally the answer to both of these questions is yes. But if the answer to the second question is "I'm not sure," then I don't take the case.

That's the luxury that plaintiffs' lawyers have: We get to pick our clients and our battles.

The ability to pick clients and cases makes plaintiffs' law more meaningful: You can choose the fight you take on. If I don't like the equities, or the client, or the case, I simply choose not to represent the client.

This is not just a matter of personal preference—it's good business. A case that fails to meet my requirements is not very valuable, and a prudent plaintiffs' lawyer should reject it.

PICKING THE TYPE OF PLAINTIFFS' LAWYER YOU WANT TO BE

How do you choose the type of plaintiffs' lawyer you'd like to be? What subject matter interests you?

Personally, I like to prosecute money laundering, fraud, and financial wrongdoing. The factual complexity and the financial component are interesting to me. Other people might enjoy technology, antitrust, consumer issues, etc.

In other words, if you are going to spend decades in a legal career, it is vital that the subject matter interests you.

There are also practical questions:

- How will you get clients for the types of cases you want?
- How much demand is there for a particular area of the law?
- How many other lawyers offer this type of service?
- Will this practice area be around for a while?
- Would you enjoy spending time with those types of clients?

Plaintiffs' law comes in so many shapes and sizes that the challenge becomes finding what is right for you.

Again, being a plaintiffs' lawyer allows me to choose which battles I fight. Once I've concluded that this plaintiff deserves justice, then I assess the facts and the law to see if there is a compelling legal case to support my equitable conclusion. In order to make this determination, I get a team of my fellow lawyers to do a deep dive to assess the viability of the legal case. I do all of this *before* I take a case.

This is what makes being a plaintiffs' lawyer so cool. We get to choose our battles. We not only shape the battlefield before the first shot is fired, but we quite literally pick which battle we want to fight.

In effect, plaintiffs' lawyers get to determine the most likely path for the defendant to lose. The defense is then left to poke holes in what we do. But of greater importance, very few defense lawyers pick the cases they work on.

Given that we get to pick our cases—in the same way prosecutors can choose which cases to prosecute—our role is *way more fun.*

Let's look at some of the major types of plaintiffs' law and talk about their positives and negatives.

Personal injury law drained me

Personal injury law is the most common type of practice that people think of when they imagine plaintiffs' law. These lawyers represent individuals who have been injured or harmed in accidents, including car wrecks.

It is not hard to have a dim view of these types of lawyers. They hawk their services on late-night TV and all those highway billboards with the easy-to-remember phone numbers.

The best personal injury lawyers play completely by the rules and find their reward in penalizing defendants who engage in conduct that causes massive injuries. Just like other plaintiffs' lawyers, their work deters wrongdoers from engaging in harmful conduct. They truly do help people who in many cases could not afford to pay a lawyer.

Make no mistake, there are many people (both ethical and unethical) making a lot of money as personal injury lawyers.

For me, I have a problem with personal injury cases. In my mind, as a personal injury lawyer I would have to make a living off of someone else's pain and suffering, which I could not be passionate about. I certainly would not want to spend a career litigating people's pain and suffering. It does not work for me at all.

Others do not look at it that way. They believe that holding people accountable for injuring innocent people and deterring those same people from engaging in injurious conduct makes society better.

It's just not for me.

How Eli's case convinced me that personal injury law is not for me

I have handled only one personal injury case in my career. A friend introduced me to a family that suffered a tragedy involving their six-year-old boy named Eli. I felt an intense emotional connection to them because Eli was just about to start first grade. At the time, my son was also about to start first grade. In fact, Eli would have been in my son's class but for the tragedy.

Eli's parents had paid for him to have private swimming lessons at summer camp in Austin. They were assured that for $175 an hour, Eli would never be in the pool without an instructor and that his lessons would be one-on-one.

Notwithstanding the promise that they made to Eli's parents, the camp instructors decided that Eli was capable enough to wait in the pool for his instructor on his own. One day, his instructor arrived to find Eli at the bottom of the pool. He had suffered an asthmatic attack. By the time Eli was pulled out of the pool and revived, he had gone up to eight minutes without oxygen, causing catastrophic brain injury.

The accident was totally avoidable and when I fully understood what happened, I was instantly angry. So I took the case on a 15 percent contingency fee because I wanted to help the family at a "friend rate."

Eventually, my team and I settled the case. In the settlement, we got Eli's family the entire insurance policy; plus the organization agreed to pay the equivalent of Eli's father's salary for ten years so that he could stay at home and take care of Eli. Over ten years later, Eli still has not fully recovered. He can only communicate with an iPad.

Even though we won "big," I have never felt so emotionally drained by a case. I remember the day-in-the-life video we made to show at the mediation. The video showed Eli shortly before the accident. He was playing in a plastic toy kitchen and selling fake hamburgers to his parents; he was so full of life. The video made everyone in the room cry—including me.

In my normal practice, I do not encounter such emotionally charged work. I prosecute business cases in which I have greater moral certainty (at least that is the case if I've done my homework), so I am on solid ground.

But a case like Eli's raises more complex moral questions, like: "Am I doing the right thing?"

I charged Eli's family a 15 percent contingent fee when virtually any other lawyer would have charged 30 or 40 percent. I tried to think of what I had done for Eli's family as a generous service that really accomplished great things. But I still came away asking myself, *Am I right to charge the family at all?*

Again, I am not making the case that what I did was right or wrong; I am just explaining what caused me to struggle. In the end, I did not feel right making any fee at all in a case with so much pain and suffering. I felt bad making any money off of a catastrophic injury.

By successfully settling the case, we were able to get the family sufficient financing to get Eli state-of-the-art rehab and many other things that insurance would not cover.

Undeniably, there was a positive result from our representation, and yet I've never done another personal injury case since then. And honestly, I don't think I ever will. But again, that was my decision. I would totally respect you if you fully thought it through and made the deliberate choice to do that kind of work for a career if you did so thoughtfully as opposed to accidentally.

This is the thought process each lawyer should go through in determining what career path to take. Would this type of work sustain you and motivate you to devote a lifetime to it? If not, then keep looking.

My friend Mark Lebovitch loves
REPRESENTING MINORITY SHAREHOLDERS

My friend Mark Lebovitch works in another area of plaintiffs' law that I sometimes also work in: asserting the rights of minority shareholders. Many of our clients are often wealthy investors, but in these cases they are still the underdogs. We stand up for them in the face of more powerful institutional forces that are trying to use their position and power solely for their own benefit.

In law school Mark attended a class in which the former chancellor of the Delaware Chancery Court, Bill Allen, talked about fiduciary duties. Unlike, say, tax law, which comes down to rules and regulations, fiduciary duty comes down to concepts, such as equity and good faith.

Mark learned that without good faith, the corporate world cannot work. A corporation is a fictional entity; it is intangible and invisible. Yet shareholders give it their (real) money on the understanding that a board of directors essentially works for their collective good in running a business. Turning the fictional business structure into a functioning corporation depends on good faith.

As soon as Mark understood that, he found the idea enthralling.

Bill Allen got Mark a chance to clerk for Judge Steve Lamb on the Delaware Chancery Court. On Mark's first day in court, he saw lawyers—good lawyers—making their case at the podium for the first time. It was a light bulb moment. Mark thought, *I want to be that guy.*

Yet Mark spent four and a half years on the defense side of securities law cases in Delaware. Then one day, he won a $900 million defense case on a technicality that left the plaintiffs with nothing. Even though Mark thought his clients should not pay for it, he knew that someone ought to … and yet they would not.

He won a big defense case, but he felt empty. Victory did not feel like victory.

Mark knew then that he did not want to be a defense lawyer for his career. In addition, he hated constantly having to either bill more per hour or work more hours to make more money (in other words, he too hated the billable hour).

In contrast, he found a plaintiffs' contingency fee practice very attractive: Plaintiffs' lawyers were paid if they created value by making money for their clients or improving governance. Mark wanted a contingency fee practice because then he could marry his payday with his client's victory.

As a result, Mark quit his BigLaw defense practice to develop a Delaware corporate governance litigation practice in a plaintiffs' firm.

Like me, Mark loves using the law to do good. We do not try to game the law for our own personal benefit. We both believe we can do well for ourselves by doing something that has true value.

We are not holier-than-thou. Mark was a securities litigator; I often represent hedge funds. We understand that what we do is not as righteous as some other fights, though Mark tells a story about coming up against a conservative defense lawyer in court who hated plaintiffs' lawyers.

During a break, she said, "My God, Mark, you really believe in this stuff, don't you?" He said, "What do you mean? I am the Thurgood Marshall for shareholder rights." It was a ludicrous comparison, and the lawyer was duly triggered. Mark pressed his point to infuriate her even more: "I'm saving the world for shareholders."

He was not going to let her mock him for doing something he believed was useful … even if it was not on the same scale as desegregating education.

Plaintiffs' law is much broader than what you've been told

I have laid out only a few cases in this chapter, but there are literally countless examples where lawyers have tried different practice areas to determine what area of the law they are passionate about.

Julia did that during law school, and many others like me have sampled practice areas during our career. But there is way, way more to plaintiffs' law than personal injury law and minority shareholders' rights.

Here's an incomplete list of some of the major areas of plaintiffs' law:

BUSINESS LITIGATION
- Antitrust
- Unfair Competition
- Business Torts
- Commercial Disputes
- Fraud Claims
- False Advertising
- Negligent Misrepresentation
- Partnership and Shareholders' Disputes
- Contract Disputes
- International Arbitration
- Professional Malpractice (legal, accounting, and valuation)
- Director and Officer Claims
- Corporate Malfeasance
- Breach of Fiduciary Duty
- Labor and Employment
- Fraudulent Transfer and Preference Claims
- Whistleblower Claims

FINANCIAL AND SECURITIES
- Securities Fraud
- Investor Rights
- Appraisal Rights

INTELLECTUAL PROPERTY
- Patent Infringement
- Copyright Infringement
- Trademark Infringement
- Trade Secrets
- Licensing Disputes

OIL AND GAS
- Royalty Disputes
- Mineral Rights

REAL ESTATE
- Appraisal Disputes
- Property Disputes
- Landlord-Tenant Disputes
- Construction Defects
- Eminent Domain
- Riparian Rights

ENVIRONMENTAL LAW
- Toxic Torts
- Environmental Contamination
- Climate Change Litigation

MASS TORTS
- Product Liability
- Pharmaceutical Injury
- Defective Medical Devices
- Asbestos/Mesothelioma
- Mass Fire Cases
- Railroad Havoc Cases
- Terrorist Events (e.g., World Trade Center bombing)
- Class Actions

PERSONAL INJURY
- Motor Vehicle Accident
- Slip and Fall
- Medical Malpractice

- Workplace Injury
- Premises Liability
- Wrongful Death
- Brain Injury
- Spinal Cord Injury
- Burn Injury
- Jones Act/Maritime
- Aviation

CIVIL RIGHTS

- Employment Discrimination
- Police Brutality
- Prisoner Rights
- Disability Rights
- Housing Discrimination
- Voting Rights
- Federal Tort Claims Act
- Section 1983 Litigation

CONSUMER PROTECTION

- Privacy and Data Security Litigation
- Consumer Fraud
- Debt Collection/Harassment
- Identity Theft
- Lemon Law
- False Advertising
- Housing Disputes
- Wage and Hour Violations
- Wrongful Termination
- Sexual Harassment
- Workplace Discrimination

Think for a second about that incredibly long list and all the important work that some of those lawyers do.

Although there are many personal injury type lawyers, there are so many more plaintiffs' lawyers doing meaningful, interesting, and important work. The problem is that you only hear about the "ambulance chasers." In part, that is due to the fact that very few, if any, of the other types of plaintiffs' lawyers advertise like personal injury lawyers do.

CHAPTER 9:

BigLaw Chooses Clients, Not Cases

IN CONTRAST TO PLAINTIFFS' LAWYERS, defense lawyers do *not* choose their cases, and have only one criterion in choosing a client:

Can this asshole pay my bill?

It doesn't matter if the client sold tobacco, opioids, or nearly destroyed the US financial system. If the client can pay the bill, legions of defense lawyers—especially BigLaw lawyers—are happy to charge thousands of hours to the client and be paid handsomely to simply delay justice and try to get the client off for the lowest number.

Don't get me wrong, defense work can be very lucrative. I just cannot see how anyone could find reward and meaning in a career devoted to representing institutions who engage in bad acts simply because it is financially rewarding. A career representing the Goliaths of the world would not sustain me. I could not be passionate about winning a defense case.

WINNING WOULD NOT BE WINNING.

I suspect that one of the reasons many defense lawyers are unhappy and suffer mental health issues is precisely because they do not get to pick the cases they work on, and as a result, they lack true meaning and reward in what they do.

In my opinion, the ability to pick your cases and clients is critical to your happiness as a lawyer.

BigLaw is virtually always on the defense side. It does not generally go after corporate wrongdoers, because it has already chosen to represent them. This is due to the fact that large corporations are the only ones that can afford to pay $2,000 an hour for legal work and pile up millions in fees.

There are so many examples of BigLaw defending bullies. In fact, in almost every single case I outlined showing you plaintiffs' lawyers as heroes, the opposing counsel was a BigLaw firm.

A prime example of BigLaw's defense of corporate bullies arises out of the 2008 financial crisis.

One of the most egregious examples of institutional wrongdoing also occurred during the 2008 financial crisis … Goldman Sachs and the Abacus case.

Goldman Sachs is one of the largest financial institutions in the world, and it routinely employs dozens of the largest BigLaw firms. And the BigLaw firms that do not work with Goldman Sachs would love to get a piece of the billions they spend with lawyers every year.

Here's what happened: Goldman Sachs was packaging and selling residential mortgage-backed securities (RMBS) to investors. But it knew that the RMBS it was selling were toxic.

The bank wasn't just trying to off-load junk assets before they collapsed in value. Goldman was also doing something even worse. It was structuring synthetic collateral debt obligations (CDO) like Abacus, which allowed its favored clients—like hedge fund Paulson & Co.—to select the worst mortgages in the portfolio, bet against them, and then sell that same product to unsuspecting investors without disclosing what it knew, much less its conflict.

In plain terms, Goldman Sachs was betting against the very investments it was marketing to its clients as solid.

That's called fraud. Dressed up in suits and spreadsheets, but fraud all the same.

It was a scandal so outrageous that even the SEC had to act. In 2010, the agency brought charges against Goldman Sachs and one of its bankers, Fabrice Tourre. The civil suit alleged that Goldman misled investors, and eventually, Goldman settled for $550 million—a large number at the time, though arguably a slap on the wrist given the damage.

But here's what often gets missed in the headlines: while the SEC grabbed attention, *it was plaintiffs' lawyers who fought in the trenches for the victims.* Several lawyers represented clients who had been tricked into investing in Abacus. They brought civil actions and fought to uncover documents and expose the playbook. These were complex cases—against a behemoth with unlimited legal resources and a playbook built around delay and denial. But they pressed forward and helped force the kind of accountability that no regulator alone could achieve.

That's the part of this work I want people to understand. It's not just about fighting bad actors—it's about fighting back when the system is tilted.

PLAINTIFFS' LAWYERS DON'T ONLY WORK FOR INDIVIDUAL JUSTICE; WE CHASE SYSTEMIC JUSTICE.

When institutions cheat and exploit, our job is to make sure they don't get away with it.

But this wasn't limited to Goldman Sachs. Almost every Wall Street bank was in the wrong during this period, and virtually every major BigLaw firm was rushing to charge them huge fees for defense.

In fact, because BigLaw makes so much money providing so many services to Wall Street banks and the rest of the corporate American giants, it is not only willing to take more of their money to defend them, it actually *can't bring a case against them.*

Preexisting client relationships create conflicts of interest that bar BigLaw from taking a case against those same interests.

If you don't know the story of the 2008 financial crisis, here it is in short:

In the years leading up to the 2008 financial crisis, banks flooded the market with residential mortgage-backed securities (RMBS)—bundles of home loans sold to investors. The idea was simple: take thousands of mortgages, pool them together, and slice them into securities that could be bought and sold. Investors got a piece of the mortgage payments, and the banks made money packaging and selling the deals.

But the system was rotten.

To keep the RMBS pipeline full, banks lowered underwriting standards. Borrowers were given loans they couldn't afford—"liar loans," no-doc loans, subprime loans with teaser rates that would reset sky-high. These risky mortgages were then stuffed into RMBS deals and labeled as safe, often earning triple-A ratings from credit agencies, who were paid by the same banks issuing the bonds to provide these bogus ratings. The ratings agencies even privately joked about their bogus ratings.

When the housing market collapsed, the RMBS fraud was exposed. Borrowers defaulted in waves. RMBS deals imploded. Pension funds, insurance companies, and institutional investors lost billions. But the real damage was systemic: These toxic assets had been woven into the global financial system.

To make matters worse, the insurance giant AIG came up with its own way to take advantage of the RMBS market: credit default swaps. They insured RMBS against defaulting. Prior to 2008 AIG and the other companies who issued credit default swaps had never paid out. In their minds, they were printing free money without risk by selling these credit default swaps.

Now we know how wrong they were.

In the years leading up to 2008, AIG alone sold hundreds of billions of dollars of credit default swaps. When savvy financial institutions realized that RMBS were a house of cards, they bought the credit default swaps in droves, betting that there would be massive defaults. They were right, and the credit default swaps turned out to be very valuable. Correspondingly, AIG was liable for hundreds of billions of dollars—and when it came time to pay out, they did not have the money.

AIG's inability to pay the holders of credit default swaps left financial institutions like Goldman Sachs unable to collect on their bet against RMBS. The government hates to upset institutions like Goldman Sachs, so guess what? Hank Paulson, a former chairman and CEO of Goldman Sachs who was then the secretary of the Treasury, decided to bail out AIG to the tune of $182 billion ... with taxpayer money.

The government's AIG bailout enabled Goldman Sachs and other opportunistic investors to reap the billions of dollars of rewards they stood to gain from their AIG-issued credit default swaps when the RMBS market melted down. (This is all described in Michael Lewis's book *The Big Short*, and the movie based on it. It is interesting to speculate why the AIG part of the story was not told in the movie.)

In the aftermath, plaintiffs' lawyers brought lawsuits against the banks, alleging that they knowingly misrepresented the quality of the mortgages they packaged and sold. The lawsuits were aimed at forcing them to either buy back the loans or pay out huge settlements. And these plaintiffs' lawyers were the primary "prosecutors" of the bad conduct.

Do you know how many banks the government criminally pursued related to the 2008 financial crisis?

Virtually none.

To be sure, the government levied penalties and fines against the institutions. But only a handful of actual people were criminally prosecuted, despite the clear criminality that had taken place.

This stuff gets me fired up. This is why I love being a plaintiffs' lawyer.

CHAPTER 10

Mcdonald's and the Magna Carta: Why Plaintiffs' Law Is Misunderstood

PLAINTIFFS' LAWYERS WERE THE ORIGINAL LAWYERS.

One of my favorite things about being a plaintiffs' lawyer is that my profession is part of a long history of fighting for justice. The roots of our work stretch back to the early days of English common law, after the Norman Conquest and long before the Magna Carta.

The history of English common law, which was the basis for American common law and the American legal system, is a long and compelling story, but I can sum it up quickly:

For centuries, there weren't different "types" of lawyers. If you were injured by another person, your only remedy was to find a lawyer who would bring an action against the person who injured you. There weren't law firms or different types of lawyers. There were only the lawyers we now call plaintiffs' lawyers.

The common law developed case by case. Lawyers and judges built the body of law we now rely on. Over time, the common law became a counterweight to power. It protected people from kings, tyrants, and anyone who tried to operate above the law.

When the Magna Carta was signed in 1215, it didn't invent this system, it reaffirmed it. The idea that justice should be available through the courts, and not at the whim of rulers, was already taking hold.

This legal tradition was imported by the United States. The founding generation was steeped in common law, and many of the leading figures were practicing lawyers. The list of founding fathers who were plaintiffs' lawyers is a Who's Who of American history: John Adams, Thomas Jefferson, Alexander Hamilton, Samuel Chase, Daniel Webster, Henry Clay, and many more.

It is not an exaggeration to say that the collective efforts of plaintiffs' lawyers laid the foundation for the modern Western world and America.

So if plaintiffs' lawyers have such an illustrious history, and do such great work now that helps so many people . . . then why don't more people understand this?

Why do plaintiffs' lawyers have such a bad reputation?

Two big reasons: coffee and commercials.

THE INFAMOUS MCDONALD'S CASE

When criticizing plaintiffs' lawyers, the most common story people reference is the McDonald's hot coffee case.

Everyone knows the basic claim: a seventy-nine-year old woman spilled coffee on herself and sued McDonald's for millions for the burn injuries she suffered.

My daughter came home from school one day and talked about it. She was fourteen, and the case is over thirty years old. She said, "You know someone won a million dollars because McDonald's served them coffee that was too hot?"

Like every case, the facts are critically important to understand the outcome.

In 1992, the plaintiff bought coffee at the McDonald's drive-thru and accidentally spilled the entire cup in her lap. The coffee soaked through her pants and caused severe third-degree burns to her thighs, buttocks, and crotch. Her injuries were so severe that she had to spend eight days in the hospital, had several skin grafts, and endured two years of medical treatment—not to mention incredible pain and suffering.

During the trial, the jury heard evidence that McDonald's required that its coffee be served at 180 to 192 degrees, which was, on average, 20 degrees hotter than typical coffee. Expert testimony was offered to show that at 190 degrees, coffee can cause third-degree burns in as little as three seconds; 180-degree coffee would take twelve to fifteen seconds, and at the more typical temperature of 160 degrees, it would take over twenty seconds of exposure to cause third-degree burns.

Of even greater significance, the jury also heard evidence that McDonald's had received over *seven hundred reports* of burns to its customers during the 1982–1992 time frame, including many severe burn injuries. Yet, McDonald's did *nothing* to change its practice of serving extra-hot coffee.

Meanwhile, other than arguing that the plaintiff was at fault for causing her own injuries, the McDonald's defense team also attempted to justify its policy of serving extra-hot coffee on the argument that its customers did not immediately consume their coffee. But the jury was shown internal McDonald's research demonstrating that McDonald's *knew* that most of its customers consumed their coffee immediately.

The case was tried to a jury in 1994. The jury awarded $200,000 in compensatory damages, which was cut to $160,000 to reflect the fact that the plaintiff was found to be 20 percent contributorily negligent.

But everyone focused on the jury's punitive damages award of $2.7 million, which was based on the revenue that McDonald's received from two days of coffee sales.

No one mentions the fact that the jury's punitive damages award was *logical*. Surely, the facts of the case supported the jury's decision to award two days of coffee sales as a penalty. Nor does anyone mention the fact that the judge later cut the punitive damages award to $480,000, which represented three times the compensatory damages award, something that is very common.

Most people think they know the McDonald's coffee case. They don't.

They roll their eyes and ask, "How could someone not know coffee is hot?" They treat the case as shorthand for greedy plaintiffs' lawyers and gullible juries. But that's because they've never seen the evidence the jury saw—or the instructions the jury followed. They've been handed a warped version of the story, and they've bought it.

The McDonald's case stands out as the poster child for tort reform. It is known to virtually everyone. And, quite frankly, law school does very little to change the impression that many have of plaintiffs' law. In fact, the negative impression of plaintiffs' lawyers is reinforced through a warped view of what happened in the McDonald's case and that view is trumpeted in tort reform campaigns.

Ambulance chasers make plaintiffs' lawyers look bad

If the ambulance-chasing attorneys you see shouting on TV about car accidents were the only people doing plaintiffs' law, then the stereotypes would be fair and I would not be doing it or advocating it.

I can't defend the people who go on TV and scream repetitive jingles trying to sear their names or phone numbers into viewers' consciousness.

Or the ones who flood your mailbox with gaudy flyers, or the ones who pay for ludicrous billboards that mock the pain and suffering of others.

I despise them more than anyone, because they make my noble profession look like clowns. I can't defend these actions, and I recognize the stain they put on my profession.

And I understand why people are repulsed by the types of lawyers who showed up in East Palestine, Ohio, handing out business cards after a train derailment spilled toxic chemicals in February 2023. Or the ones who raced to the fires in Hawaii and

California, callously looking for clients. That's terrible.

Every profession has its black sheep, and they are ours.

All I can do is be as ethical and upstanding as I can be, and maybe write a book like this to give the best case possible for the whole profession.

And, of course, my phone number is 512-647-6100—*not* 1-800-GET-MONEY.

CHAPTER 11

Why I Love Plaintiffs' Law

FOR ME, THE JOY OF PLAINTIFFS' LAW HAS SEVERAL COMPONENTS:

1. IMPACT:

Winning feels like winning: When I was a prosecutor, I put drug offenders behind bars. It was the "correct" outcome, but it didn't make me feel great. Winning cases that I truly believe in brings me immense satisfaction. Winning cases that matter to me allow me to fight for the victim and recover damages for the injuries they have suffered.

2. COMPLEXITY:

I enjoy solving complex legal puzzles: In complex financial litigation, I get to satisfy my insatiable thirst to solve challenging legal puzzles. I call this "three-dimensional chess." And I love to play three-dimensional chess against the smartest lawyers and win.

3. WIN-WIN OUTCOME:

My clients win with me: When I win cases that I have chosen to pursue, I get to share in the victory via my success fee. I get to partner with my clients and share the victory with the client.

4. SENSE OF JUSTICE AND PUNISHING WRONGDOERS:

I get to fight bullies: I have a strong sense of justice and I hate bullies. It is often more rewarding and meaningful when I win cases against the Goliaths and make them pay. Making them pay serves as both punishment for the past and (hopefully) a deterrent in the future. I love taking cases with a clear wrongdoer and I'm able to not only help my client, but right a wrong and possibly even ensure that others are deterred from committing that wrong again.

Success fee plaintiffs' law is the only type of law I'm aware of that allows me to experience all of these components. Some cases have more of some than the other, but no other kind of law allows for all four.

The highlights of my career are the cases when I was able to make a difference in someone's life. This happens most often when I represent a single person. Truthfully, some of these cases were more modest in dollars.

Marrying my economics to the outcome of the cases I pursue allows me to truly partner with my clients. We win or lose together. When they win, I get paid.

There is also true reward and satisfaction in forcing bullies to pay for their wrongdoing. This is why I like to describe what I do as "fighting bullies." That is what representing the Davids of the world against the Goliath institutional wrongdoers means to me.

Some people say that it's not possible to change people's behavior. In their view, greedy people are always going to be greedy. I agree that greed is not going away anytime soon, but for sure there is a deterrent effect associated with plaintiffs' work. Through plaintiffs' work, you can change behavior and you can force people to rethink their actions, oftentimes for the benefit of society.

Financial litigation is a passionate pursuit for me. For you to truly love the law—especially plaintiffs' law—you need to find the type of plaintiffs' law that stokes your passion.

The way I like to think about it is that most bad financial actors are motivated by money. Money is their language. Making greedy Goliaths pay in their own language is the best way to change their behavior, and it gives me true reward. I hate bullies, so I love holding them accountable in their own language—money. I could not find reward and satisfaction representing those same bullies.

What sustains you and fires you up? What wrongful conduct and bad actors would motivate you to pursue a legal career against them for decades?

There's not a right or wrong answer here; what is exciting and meaningful differs between people.

I know the stories about taking on the tobacco or opioid industry seem bigger than life. I understand that, and this sort of mass tort law is not a field I went into either.

Let me share with you a few of my own stories about justice and my efforts to change the lives of real people.

The worst kind of greed: The Grey Goose vodka case

Early in my career as a plaintiffs' lawyer, I was approached by a guy named Bruce Bakerman. Bruce was no one's idea of the "little guy" who gets screwed by the system; he was a successful business executive and a Harvard-trained lawyer. He had been treated terribly by his employer but could not get anyone to hold them accountable.

Bruce did not get screwed because he was dumb. He was a smart guy. He did not get screwed because he got greedy. He was a diffident man who spent his time caring for his elderly mother.

He got screwed because a handful of executives with a shit-ton of money decided to take money from Bruce to add to their own piles.

That's where we came along.

Bruce worked as assistant general counsel for Sidney Frank Importing Co (SFIC), the holding company of Grey Goose Bottling (GGB), which made the popular vodka. Bruce owned a 10 percent equity stake in Grey Goose Bottling, but none in Sidney Frank Importing. When the CEO and executives who ran Sidney Frank negotiated a $2.3 billion sale to Bacardi, they sold both SFIC and GGB, but they allocated just $19 million of the value to GGB (equal to its outstanding debt at the time), and the remaining $2.819 billion was allocated to SFIC.

It was obvious that the GGB assets were worth many multiples of the $19 million allocation. GGB owned the recipe for the vodka, the main bottling plant in Cognac, France, and the distribution rights in France and many parts of Asia and Australia. Meanwhile, SFIC owned the distribution rights in North America and Europe (except France). Without GGB's assets, Bacardi would never have paid $2.3 billion for just SFIC.

The greedy executives who decided to value GGB at just $19 million effectively assigned Bruce's stake a zero valuation.

They didn't care about the GGB allocation because they held shares in both entities, while Bruce exclusively held shares in GGB. That meant their decision solely harmed Bruce. To make matters worse, by screwing Bruce they got an incremental bump in their profits from the sale.

In order to conclude their secret negotiations with Bacardi, they needed Bruce's consent to the GGB allocation. After Bruce initially balked, the executives presented Bruce with three options:

- He could sign the deal, accept the unfair valuation, get $1 million, and leave his job;
- He could sign the deal, get $700K and keep his $300K-a-year job; or
- He could refuse to sign the deal, be sued, possibly disbarred and imprisoned and get no money.

Like a BigLaw exploding offer, the bastards gave Bruce thirty minutes to decide. Because he cared for his elderly mother, he chose door number two. He signed the consent and cashed the $700K check.

But he knew he had been screwed. He also knew lots of lawyers, but every one Bruce contacted turned down his case. He had signed the consent and cashed the check. It was a slam dunk for the company.

Bruce eventually made his way to me, and his story pissed me off. I approach all of my cases from a fairness vantage point. And the lack of fairness in Bruce's case stank.

My partners and I searched for a way to help Bruce using the Delaware doctrine of "entire fairness." The doctrine exists specifically to protect minority shareholders if majority shareholders try to screw them. That sounded pretty spot-on, but the aha moment came when we realized that it protected even shareholders who have consented to a transaction and received the benefits of it. If the transaction is objectively not entirely fair in process or substance, then the beneficiary of the unfair transaction can be held liable for breach of fiduciary duty.

We could not have written the law better if we'd written it ourselves. In ruling against the company's motion to dismiss, former Delaware Chancellor William Chandler found the company respected no process at all. Not only that, he called the allocation of $19 million in equity to Grey Goose in a $2.3 billion deal "ludicrous." That is strong language coming from the bench.

The settlement we won for Bruce changed his life. He will never have to work again. He and his mom went off to enjoy themselves in Florida, while my team and I got our first taste of justice fighting bullies—with a nice contingent fee kicker.

Let me tell you: That is a highly addictive combination.

If you're wondering why Bruce signed a deal he knew was wrong, the answer is simple: He was intimidated. He was in over his head, and he was dealing with bullies. And remember, Bruce was a smart guy with a Harvard Law degree.

If it could happen to him, it could happen to anyone.

And it does. Every day.

If you are wondering why no other lawyer took the case, to us the answer seems clear: None of them had the guts. Most lawyers are risk averse, but we love taking calculated risks. And, as Judge Garza would have observed, the case was about the

Sidney Frank executives fucking over Bruce.

And we love taking down bullies.

Playing complex 3D chess: The Renren case

My good friend Alex Shoghi from Oasis Management came to me in 2018 and said, "I'm looking at a deal that stinks." Oasis had invested millions in Renren, a Chinese social media company turned investment fund whose majority shareholders— SoftBank and two Chinese nationals, Joe Chen and David Chao—were proposing a deal that would effectively spin off what could be objectively valued at $1.5 billion in assets.

Those assets were not operating companies or things that are tough to value, but equity in other companies, including a fairly large stake in a company called SoFi, an online lending company that had done quite well.

Instead of paying for the $1.5 billion in assets that they spun off, the controlling shareholders got a valuation from Duff & Phelps that was obviously bogus. The "appraisal" concluded that the assets were worth only $500 million. They offered the minority shareholders their 30 percent share of the $500 million in the form of a dividend. Of course, if the assets were in fact worth $500 million, then the transaction might well have been proper. But the valuation was off by $1 billion.

And they knew that the Duff & Phelps $500 million valuation was totally off base. We later discovered a contemporaneous internal Excel spreadsheet that the defendants prepared showing that the spun-off assets were in fact worth $1.5 billion.

To make matters worse, in the Renren case, the defendants were not even using their own money to fund the minority shareholders' dividend. They took $134 million from the company's bank account to pay the minority their dividend. Effectively they were using company money to pay the minority shareholders to walk off with $1.5 billion in assets. The only problem with that was that the minority shareholders owned their share of that cash too.

The majority shareholders owned 70 percent of the company and they were essentially stealing the minority's remaining 30 percent with money from Renren's bank account. Meanwhile, they were paying the minority only their 30 percent share of one-third of the actual value.

They did not need the money. They were just doing it because they had the power to do it.

Shoghi wanted to pursue a claim against the majority shareholders, but it was very complicated. Because the fiduciary duties owed by the majority shareholders to a Cayman company are governed by Cayman law, even in the US courtroom, we had to proceed under Cayman law. More importantly, as a gateway issue we had to get jurisdiction over the subsidiary of a Japanese bank, SoftBank, and two Chinese individuals.

These two issues (derivative standing and personal jurisdiction) presented a very complex three-dimensional chess game. Exactly the sort of puzzle that I love to solve.

The founders of Renren (Chen and Chao) had rung the bell on the New York Stock Exchange when they did their secondary offering in 2011. They raised $800 million for a 10 percent stake in Renren, which was supposed to be the next Facebook of China. They failed at the business, but they started buying private equity interests in companies, including SoFi, and those underlying investments became valuable.

We sued them in New York State Supreme Court for breach of fiduciary duty. We sought derivative standing under Cayman law. We also alleged that the defendants had purposefully availed themselves of a New York forum in carrying out the very transaction at issue—so-called specific jurisdiction.

In response, Chen and Chao argued that the New York courts had no jurisdiction over them. Additionally, they argued that we lacked standing to pursue a claim on Renren's behalf.

In his jurisdictional challenge, Chen contended that he was a Chinese citizen with zero contacts to the US. In support, he put in an affidavit stating that he had not resided in the US since 2004 and that he never had a bank account in the state of New York. Of course, these self-serving allegations were his "proof" that he was not subject to jurisdiction.

But Chen's jurisdictional contentions were not true. We discovered that the underlying securities in Renren were American Depositary Receipts, or ADRs. In order for a foreign company to sell ADRs on a US exchange, Renren needed to have a banking relationship with an American depository bank. In this case, its depository bank was Citibank in New York.

In order for the defendants to get shares in their new Cayman company (the one they were sending Renren's valuable assets to), they had to make an election and send that election to Renren's lawyers in New York City. Additionally, when the defendants paid the special dividend to the minority shareholders, the $134 million came from Renren's New York bank. The underlying transaction happened almost entirely in New York.

In order to establish standing, we relied on an 1843 English case called *Foss v. Harbottle*, which controls whether a minority shareholder has the right to bring a derivative action under English/Cayman law. Standing is often a very complex issue under US law. Here we were fighting a standing issue that arose under Cayman law—making it even more complex.

There had been twenty-one prior cases in New York in which minority shareholders attempted to bring a derivative case under Cayman law pursuant to *Foss v. Harbottle*, and all of them had failed. There was literally only one previous case in which a derivative plaintiff had successfully asserted standing in a US courtroom under Cayman law. To make matters worse, there were no Cayman cases addressing the issue at all.

Nonetheless, we were able to establish derivative standing under Cayman law. In fact, we won the issue on appeal in New York's Appellate Division, which gave us the only appellate victory on derivative standing in a US court ever in US litigation history.

So we won on jurisdiction and we won on derivative standing, which empowered a minority shareholder like Shoghi to bring a claim on the company's behalf.

A derivative action is the legal vehicle where a minority shareholder can bring what is otherwise a company claim when the company is under control of the bad guys and they will not sue themselves. The law allows the minority shareholders to sue them on the company's behalf when that situation arises.

Then we proceeded to discovery. We quickly learned that Chen, who claimed to live in China and argued that he had nothing to do with the United States, was renting a house in Arizona. Additionally, he was selling some of the underlying assets and having the cash deposited in a New York bank account. That looked bad and caused us concern about collectability. We were worried that they were going to dissipate all of the assets they had taken from Renren and that we would get a judgment at the end and have no way to collect it.

We went back to court and said, "Judge, they're selling the assets they took and there may be nothing left at the end of the day. This is unfair. Please stop them." We asked the judge to issue an injunction to order them to take all the cash they got from the sales and put it into the registry of the court in New York and to order them to cease further sales.

At the hearing I told the judge, "Mr. Chen lied to you." The judge said, "Tell me about that."

I said, "He told you he didn't have a New York bank account, but the proceeds of the sales of the misappropriated Renren assets were directed to a New York bank account in Mr. Chen's personal name with a New York address."

I said, "In addition, he declared in his affidavit at the outset of this case that he was a Chinese resident who had not resided in the US since 2004. We can now show you that he was leasing a house in Arizona when he made that declaration under oath."

We were on a Zoom call with about fifty defense lawyers. I had argued only for the lesser remedy of an injunction, which would prevent only future sales of these assets; I did not argue for a prejudgment writ of attachment, which is a much more onerous remedy.

At the conclusion of my argument, I felt that things had gone well. To my surprise, the judge denied my request for an injunction. I was puzzled at this ruling because I thought I had won the hearing.

Then the judge said, "I'm granting a writ of attachment and I will upload an order this afternoon." The judge then hit "leave" from the Microsoft Teams meeting, leaving all fifty lawyers looking at one another. It was a mic drop moment.

The defense lawyers looked dumbfounded, and my team and I were texting each other, "What in the hell just happened?"

We had just won more than I had asked for in the hearing, and the court then ordered the onerous remedy of a prejudgment writ of attachment that we had not even pressed at argument.

As we soon found out when we received the court's written order, the judge had ordered the defendants to return the proceeds of the stock sales, which were sitting in a bank account in China. And he further barred the defendants from selling any of the remaining assets. It was better than a home run. It was a grand slam.

Shortly thereafter, we settled the case for $300 million, which was directly paid to Renren's 30 percent minority shareholders. It was the same as if we had recovered the $1 billion of value taken from the company as it translated to the minority shareholders, which was the exact number that the minority shareholders lost in connection with the transaction: 30 percent of $1 billion.

I am very proud of the result my team achieved in the Renren case. It is probably the best example of a three-dimensional chess victory in my career.

PART 3:

The Business of Law

CHAPTER 12

The Biggest Secret in Law: Rainmakers Rule

Mark Lanier didn't go to Harvard. He went to Texas Tech. That didn't stop him from racking up $20 billion in verdicts—and becoming the lawyer other lawyers call to try their cases.

Like Lanier, some of the most successful trial lawyers had unremarkable credentials. Gerry Spence went to the University of Wyoming College of Law. Clarence Darrow had one year of law school and then apprenticed his way to a dominant legal career.

Of course, there are plenty of lawyers with great credentials too. Steve Susman went to UT, graduated first in his class, and clerked at the Supreme Court. David Boies graduated at the top of his class at Yale Law School.

They all took different routes but they achieved the same results. They succeeded because they all found ways to distinguish themselves and stand out to clients. They became rainmakers.

There is a hard truth about private law practice—one that's rarely taught in school and often realized much later in a lawyer's career. The truth is this:

The lawyers who bring in clients—the rainmakers—control the profession.

In every firm, regardless of size or structure, there are two types of partners. First, there are *origination partners* or *rainmakers*, who bring in business. Then, there are *service partners*, who work on that business. Rainmakers are not necessarily the most brilliant or academically successful. They are the lawyers who generate the business.

Everyone works for the rainmakers.

What is rainmaking?

Let's be clear: Rainmaking isn't just sales. Sales is a component of rainmaking, but rainmaking is a comprehensive strategy. It is dynamic and ongoing. Client origination or business development is the process by which lawyers go about attracting and keeping clients. The ones who succeed at this process are called rainmakers.

Trust me: You want to be a rainmaker.

Rainmaking is about relationships. It's about building a reputation, a skill set, and a network of people who can help guide work to you. The best rainmakers draw clients because they are able to connect with them and solve their problems.

One of the most effective client development strategies that I've found over the years is comprehensive preparation. Many lawyers like to talk about their firms and their past conquests. Don't get me wrong, that stuff is important.

But clients are always impressed if you have done enough homework to show that you have thought about their case and that you have a preliminary strategy in mind. They want to see that you are focused on achieving a result and solving their problem.

Rainmakers don't just sell services. They own outcomes. The more outcomes a given rainmaker can achieve, the greater the rainmaker's power to keep and retain business. Translated, this means that it is critically important for a lawyer to achieve results.

Clients want someone that gives them confidence. Having already achieved the same or similar goals for someone else gives clients the reassurance that you can and will achieve those results again—for them.

I like to say that getting my first nine-figure case was hard, but as time has passed, it has become easier and easier. Now I get ten-figure cases fairly often. Why? Because I have a long track record of winning those cases for clients.

In short, rainmaking is the most important function in any law firm. Without a client, what good is the best legal team? My friend Alan Brown once told me many years ago:

"Good lawyers are a dime a dozen. The real diamonds in the legal world are the ones who bring in clients—the rainmakers."

What makes a rainmaker?

Rainmakers are not born. They're built—deliberately, patiently, and strategically. The best ones tend to share certain traits—few of which show up on a résumé.

Great rainmakers:

- **Build reputations, not resumes.** They don't chase credentials—they create value.
- **Invest in relationships.** Not transactionally, but consistently, with thoughtfulness and purpose.
- **Treat clients as partners.** Not paychecks. Not problems. Partners. They listen, they empathize, they collaborate, and they obtain results.
- **Own the problem.** They take responsibility and deliver solutions.
- **Go the extra mile.** They look around corners, think two moves ahead, and find ways to add value even when not asked.
- **Are relentlessly responsive.** They return calls and emails—*fast*. Even when they don't have the answer yet. Clients remember that.
- **Know what they know.** They don't bluff. When the issue's outside their lane, they bring in the right person.
- **Get results and broadcast them.** The absolute best calling card is a successful result.
- **Think long-term, not short-term.** By treating clients well over the long term, you will enjoy far more success than focusing on how to maximize your short-term opportunity.

These aren't soft skills. These are strategic differentiators. They're how you build leverage.

Obviously, there are so many types of rainmakers, and whole books could be written on the different types and their approaches.

But this list is a good start, and now that you understand how the game is played, you will be better prepared to win it.

My approach to rainmaking

Most rainmakers are very protective of their client relationships and approach client development on their own. I am not.

Early in my career, being part of a team of lawyers pitching business was incredibly helpful to becoming a rainmaker myself. By watching senior lawyers deal with clients, I was able to learn my own style. I adopted some of the approaches that I liked best and added my own elements to create my own style.

My firm collaborates on client development. Like everything else that we do, it is important to assemble a team from the outset. We then empower the entire team and each take on a role. This way, when we pitch a case, we all pitch it together. We share the rainmaking responsibility so that younger lawyers can learn how to pursue client development. This is how I learned to become a rainmaker, and this is how we teach younger lawyers at my firm the rainmaking ropes.

Regardless of whether a rainmaker can bring in work without a team, it takes a team to actually do the work. Most significant legal matters—especially the ones worth chasing—require a team of people with complementary skills, experience, and expertise. The rainmaker's job is not over once the client engages the firm; it is then important for that rainmaker to lead the team effectively while managing the client relationship with clarity and confidence.

In other words, rainmakers don't just bring in the work; they orchestrate the result, and I achieve this by having my team involved in the whole process.

That's the model: the rainmaker as coach and strategist. Someone who interfaces constantly between the client and the team—translating needs and solving problems. If the team is cohesive enough, then multiple lawyers can joint-venture the client-facing role. In other words, a team can perform the rainmaking role.

And it's not just lawyers who make things happen. At the best-run firms, the optimal results come from teams that function at every level. That includes legal assistants and associates who handle details most clients will never see—but who are absolutely essential to making sure things go right.

I have worked with exceptional assistants—people whose judgment and hard work have been every bit as critical as that of the lawyers in the room. And many of my former associates have been elevated to partner over the years.

When I'm at my best, it's because I have a team around me that's locked in and focused. We win together through collaboration.

I see rainmaking the same way.

LAW SCHOOL SUCCESS DOES NOT EQUATE TO CAREER SUCCESS

It is counterintuitive to law students and even law faculty, but succeeding at their game does not even remotely guarantee success as a practicing lawyer. Law school rewards memorization and mastery of theory. Ultimately, law school is a theoretical boot camp that has real value—particularly early in your career.

But academic success is just the ante to get into the game. It doesn't predict who wins it. Succeeding in the real world requires something else.

You've probably heard the old adage: "A students become professors or judges, B students work for A students, and C students run the world." It's glib, but there's a kernel of truth in it. Academic success often rewards a different skill set than what is needed to succeed at the rainmaking game.

Long-term career success, especially in plaintiffs' law, rewards a different set of traits: judgment, hustle, grit, and people skills. As a result, it's often the scrappy, less-pedigreed lawyer who learns how to bring in clients.

Some of the most academically gifted people I've known have achieved only modest success in private practice. They're brilliant—but often anonymous. Why? Because rainmaking isn't about knowing the most law. It's about becoming the trusted first call when something important happens.

Most students think their credentials will carry them. They believe clients will "come in time." They assume their pedigree alone will be obvious and rewarded. It's a comforting myth. But it's not how the real world works. You can be top of your class, on Law Review, or even a Supreme Court clerk—and still find yourself answering to someone with less impressive credentials, but with a solid book of business.

The legal industry doesn't run on pedigrees and academic accomplishments. It runs on trust and results. How you go about attaining the reputation is up to you. But knowing that this is something you need to work toward is perhaps the best piece of advice I could give to any young lawyer.

Lots of students get good grades. Rainmakers get results.

The real-world power structure

Even partnerships are pyramids when it comes to the power structure.

At the bottom are the partners who don't have their own clients. And at the top are the handful of lawyers with clients. They are the ones who decide what gets worked on, who gets hired, and what gets paid.

Rainmakers ultimately decide your hours. Your bonus. Your track. Your future.

You're not truly part of a partnership if you have no stake in the relationships that sustain the business. Clients equal power. This is possibly the most important lesson you will learn about your legal career, so pay attention:

If you don't have your own clients, then your real clients are the lawyers who do.

CHAPTER 13:

How Money Works in Law

HOW LAW FIRMS ACTUALLY MAKE MONEY

Next time you visit a law firm, especially a BigLaw firm, take a look at the art, the glass, and the giant floral displays in reception and ask yourself, *Who's paying for all this?*

Clients, of course.

The legal industry is big business. Legal services contributed $397 Billion to the US GDP in 2024. And every single dollar led back ultimately to someone somewhere cutting a check to a lawyer.

As I said before, law school does not tell you much about the business of law. And to be honest, lawyers generally do not understand it themselves.

For example, most young lawyers give no thought to:

- How law firms make money
- How to figure out their value to their employer
- How to tell if their firm is doing well
- How debt impacts a law firm
- How to understand what a firm's business model is, and how they fit in

- How partners make money in a law firm

Young lawyers are like most people. They see the high-end office space and assume the firm is doing well. But they have no idea how law firm economics work. They don't know how the firm makes money, what its future looks like, or how close it might be to collapse.

And make no mistake—*some firms are closer to collapse than they look.*

How clients pay

To understand a law firm's financial health—and your place in it—you need to understand how it makes money. That means knowing how the firm charges for its services.

There are several basic models:

- **The billable hour** (charging for time);
- **Milestone payments** (payments due on certain events);
- **Flat fees or subscription fees**; and/or
- **The success fee or contingent fee** (charging for results, often called contingency or performance-based billing)

Most BigLaw firms rely almost entirely on the billable hour. On the other end of the spectrum are firms that work exclusively on a success fee. And some firms use a hybrid or mixed-fee model: blending a success fee with other guaranteed payments.

To accurately judge the financial situation of a prospective employer, you need a basic understanding of a law firm's financial model and how a given firm charges for its work. And frankly, the manner in which a firm charges for its services can tell you a lot about a firm's ethos.

Most law firms bill their clients on one of two basic models: charging by time (the billable hour) or charging by results (contingency or success fee).

There is a hybrid variation in which the client is charged either a fixed set of fees (say monthly or quarterly) or a reduced percentage of hourly fees in addition to a success fee, which is an agreed percentage or fixed amount that is payable upon a favorable outcome and/or milestones. This hybrid model is referred to as "mixed-fee" or hybrid billing. And there are countless ways to set up a hybrid model.

THE BILLABLE HOUR AND ITS
MANY FLAWS

Lawyers didn't always bill by the hour. They used to charge flat fees—simple, predictable, and tied to the task. But in the 1940s, the American Bar Association began encouraging hourly billing. Why? Jealousy. Dentists had figured out how to make more money charging by the hour, and lawyers didn't like playing second fiddle.

So lawyers adopted the billable hour. Not because it was fairer. Not because it helped clients. But because it maximized revenue. Lawyers wanted to live like dentists.

The billable hour eliminates the lawyer's risk. But it also kills alignment with the client. It rewards inefficiency. The longer something takes, the more the firm earns. The more people staffed on a task, the bigger the bill.

Even worse, once an hourly lawyer actually achieves the client's goal—by resolving the case—they stop making money. The client wants a favorable outcome as fast as possible. But hourly fee lawyers are incentivized to drag things out and maximize hours. There is an economic conflict of interest between the lawyer and the clients.

From the law firm's business perspective, hourly billing is much easier. It creates a steady, predictable income stream. There are no huge peaks or valleys. BigLaw firms can look at their last few months of billings and confidently project revenue forward. It's a financial model built for stability—at least for the firm—and at least for now.

In many of the complex cases my firm handles, the defense is paid out of liability insurance policies that are self-eroding. "Self-eroding" means every dollar spent on a covered defendant's legal fees reduces the amount of insurance left to fund a settlement. The policy is essentially a melting ice cube. Every hour billed by defense counsel reduces the pot of insurance.

In fact, it's common to see large defense firms burn through tens of millions of dollars from these insurance towers. Why? Because the insurers know the insurance proceeds will be spent either on defense costs or a settlement—so they have every incentive to run up the fees first. From the defense lawyer's perspective, they might as well extract every dollar they can before turning over the leftovers to the plaintiff.

At mid-tier firms, the incentives can be even worse. These firms often need the revenue more, and the billable hour becomes a lifeline. In those situations, a defense lawyer might consciously or subconsciously extend litigation just to keep the revenue flowing. Settling too early—even when it's a smart move for the client—can actually hurt the firm financially.

That's how warped the incentives can get. A weak lawyer can milk a bad case just to protect their annuity. And while contingency models have their flaws too—yes, they're money-driven—at least they're money-driven in the direction of a result, which is what the client wants.

So if you're still wondering why the billable hour is broken, it comes down to this: It rewards time, not results. It thrives on inefficiency. And it turns litigation into a business model designed to serve the firm—not the client.

The pure success fee model

The success fee model is the polar opposite of the hourly fee model. Here, the lawyer gets paid only if they win. Payment is tied to outcome—not time. And that's the beauty of it: The lawyer and the client both want the same thing—success.

It's a much better alignment of interests. No one is billing hours to keep the lights on. Everyone is pushing toward a result.

But while hourly billing puts all the risk on the client, the pure success fee model puts all the risk on the lawyer. And let's be honest—most lawyers don't like that. Lawyers are risk averse by nature. That's why many shy away from contingency work. They don't want to front the cost of litigation or gamble on the outcome.

Unlike the hourly fee model, contingent fee lawyering can be exciting. Unlike the risk-free, predictable BigLaw revenue model, a contingent fee lawyer can truly strike it rich—like a wildcatter in the oil patch. Every day the contingent fee lawyer comes to work could be a jackpot. Like the wildcatter, the contingent fee lawyer can also drill a dry hole. It is exciting—but it is also risky.

That risk hits hardest at the point of resolution. Because even in a contingency fee case, the client holds all the settlement authority. And while the client shares in the outcome, they don't share in the burdens of continued litigation. So, when the client says no to a deal, it's the lawyer who absorbs a disproportionate share of the consequences.

Imagine this: A defendant offers $50 million to settle a $200 million case. The client refuses anything under $75 million. Fair enough—it's their call. But if the lawyer is working on a 40 percent contingency, they're now forced to walk away from a $20 million fee. And now the lawyer is looking at months or even years of additional work to chase a bigger number. And, if they lose? The potential $20 million fee vanishes completely.

The client has minimal downside. The lawyer is all in.

That imbalance can strain even the best relationships. The client doesn't bear the grind of extended litigation. The lawyer does. And when the client rejects a deal the lawyer recommended, it's not just frustrating—it's costly.

That's the tension built into the pure contingency fee model. It creates alignment on outcome, but not always on timing. And when things drag on, that friction becomes real.

But here's why I still prefer it: I'd rather be compensated for results than time. Results are usually the by-product of hard work and sound strategy—but sometimes, they come from insight. A single *eureka* moment can completely transform a case.

So let me ask: If I waste two weeks chasing a dead end, should the client pay for that? Of course not. But if I come up with a game-changing idea while walking my dog—

one that earns the client tens of millions of dollars—shouldn't I be compensated for the value I created, not the fifteen minutes it took to create it?

That's what the success fee model gets right. It rewards outcomes, not effort. And that's all clients really care about.

The hybrid deal: Sharing risk, aligning interests

Hybrid deals are the most flexible—and in many ways, the best of both worlds. They recognize the realities on both sides: The client doesn't want to pay the lawyer endlessly without results, and the lawyer doesn't want to carry all the risk all the time.

At their core, hybrid deals blend the two major models:

- **A fixed component** (usually flat fees or milestone payments), and
- **A success fee** (paid upon achieving a defined outcome).

That fixed component gives the lawyer stability—funds to keep the case moving, cover litigation costs, and stay engaged. It also gives the client budget clarity. They know what they're committing to up front.

The success fee creates alignment. It gives the lawyer skin in the game and ties compensation to actual performance. Most importantly, it ensures both sides are working toward the same goal—a result.

And here's where hybrid deals fix one of the biggest flaws in pure contingency fee arrangements: settlement decision-making.

In a pure contingency case, the client controls settlement but doesn't suffer the same consequence if they do not make the right decision. If a client turns down a reasonable settlement offer, the burden falls entirely on the lawyer to press on. But in a hybrid deal, the client continues to finance the litigation going forward via future installments or milestone fees. That means the client must share the financial burden of saying no to a reasonable settlement.

In other words, hybrid deals align incentives by encouraging the result via a success fee but also keep the client's settlement authority in check by forcing the client to pay for continued litigation. This means that a client can't just reject a settlement offer without consequence. If they want to keep litigating, they have to help carry the load.

For me, hybrid deals often offer the best of both worlds. They best balance the interests of the lawyer and the client and create the best alignment of interest.

CHAPTER 14

Litigation Finance: A New Pestilence

How BigLaw masquerades as plaintiffs' law

For years, the only real alternative for a client that was unwilling or unable to pay an hourly fee for a plaintiffs' case was an alternative fee, meaning a contingency fee. For hourly fee lawyers with clients who could not or did not want to pay hourly fees, this was a growing problem. Many of those lawyers were unwilling to work on an alternative fee. Absent a solution to this problem, those lawyers would lose clients to contingency fee firms.

And along came a solution to this problem in the form of litigation finance. In simple terms, litigation finance works like this: A client wants to hire a firm (oftentimes a second- or third-tier BigLaw firm that does not regularly practice plaintiffs' law), but cannot afford to pay the firm's hourly fees.

Meanwhile, the firm will not do a contingency fee, either because they do not like the case enough or because they are not willing to take the risk, or both. In order to keep the work, the hourly fee law firm "shops" the case to litigation finance firms based on the understanding that the firm keeps the case and the funder pays its fees. If a funder violates this unwritten "rule," and tries to move the case to a better law firm or one willing to work on an alternative fee, then the referring law firm will not come back to the funder a second time.

The client generally trusts their lawyer, so they allow the litigation finance firm to fund the lawyer's hourly fee budget without recourse, meaning the client is not obligated to repay the litigation funding unless they win. In return for the risk the funder takes by advancing the loan on a nonrecourse basis, it gets priority repayment on the results of the litigation at a multiple of its investment dollars.

Here's an example of how it works in general: The hourly fee firm proposes a budget of, say, $10 million to handle a $100 million case. The funder proposes to finance the lawyer's fees on a nonrecourse basis, and in exchange the funder gets the first dollars out at a multiple. For simplicity in this example, let's assume the multiple is 3X.

So, the funder puts up $10 million and the case is lost, then the client owes nothing. But if the case is settled for $50 million, the funder gets $30 million (3X) and the client gets $20 million. Again, this arrangement makes more sense on the plaintiff's side, because a successful plaintiff receives a financial award that can go toward paying back the litigation finance.

What many people don't realize is that in many of these cases the funder gets paid *more* than what a contingency fee lawyer would have charged. Oftentimes the funder ends up with more than 50 percent of the economics of a case (meaning the client gets less than 50 percent of the outcome), while contingency fee lawyers rarely charge more than 40 percent (meaning the client gets at least 60 percent of the outcome).

Just like a contingent fee representation, the client is not paying his lawyer. But the lawyer still gets to bill hourly fees and the funder foots the bill. In return, the funder gets a premium in the form of a multiple.

This arrangement incentivizes funders to overfund, because the more they fund, the greater their return. Of course, the hourly fee lawyer is more than happy to overbill the case, which is obviously in the lawyer's and the funder's interest. The lawyer's excess bills actually allow the funder to earn an even greater return. If the litigation budget is $5 million, the funders might tell them, "Let's make it $10 million." They are not being generous. The more money they put in, the bigger the figure on which their return is based.

Litigation finance is also used to fund hybrid deals. In those instances, the client borrows money from the litigation financer to pay the fixed portion of the hybrid deal. That effectively means the client is then paying two success fees: one to the lawyer and another to the funder. Again, going to a high-quality law firm willing to take the risk itself reduces the ultimate amount the client has to pay.

Litigation finance is a bit like health care. The people consuming the services (the clients) are not really worried about the fees they incur because they are not paying them directly and they are not at risk if the case goes to hell in a handbasket. If that happens, the funder takes the loss. And if they win and the funder gets their share of the fees, who cares, right? Wrong: The economics are virtually always worse for the client who utilizes litigation finance rather than the client who just hires a high-quality contingency fee lawyer directly.

Meanwhile, the contingency fee lawyer is incentivized to earn the success as soon as possible, which aligns with the client's desired timing as well. These incentives are absent when a litigation funder enters the equation and allows the hourly fee lawyer to extend and overbill (because again, it is in both the lawyer's and the funder's interest). In other words, unlike contingency fee lawyers, hourly fee lawyers using litigation finance have no incentive to resolve the case.

I see litigation finance as a pestilence.

Litigation finance skews the legal market. It funds inferior lawyers who are unwilling to bet on themselves and, in many cases, lawyers who frankly have no business taking a plaintiff's case.

The funders are not even betting on the ability of a particular set of lawyers. Their bet is a matter of pure math. The funders charge enough of a premium that they can afford to lose some cases and still make a killing. The inferior lawyers will benefit regardless of the outcome.

My law firm competes with litigation funding. If I quote a standard 35 percent contingency fee on a $100 million case and win every penny, my firm would get $35 million and the client would get $65 million. Cases rarely settle for 100 percent of the damage model.

Let's say the same case is settled for $50 million. My firm would get $17.5 million and the client gets the balance: $32.5 million.

Now, let's say the client obtained $10M of litigation funding. For that same $50 million settlement, the client would get no more than $20 million.

That is the equivalent of paying a contingency fee in excess of 50 percent—which no contingency firm would ever (or could ever) charge.

Many clients choose to use litigation funding so they can afford to hire a BigLaw firm to pursue plaintiffs' litigation. That choice is based on the misguided belief that a big hourly fee firm must be better at prosecuting a plaintiffs' case than a plaintiffs' boutique firm.

I could not disagree more.

The reality is that most BigLaw firms have no business handling a plaintiffs' case.

Litigation finance exists for one reason: law firms suck at running themselves. Entrepreneurs who saw a chance to make money from BigLaw started paying for litigation in Australia in the 1990s, and it really took off in the UK around 2005. It is no coincidence that both those jurisdictions lacked contingency fee lawyers until recently.

Over twenty years later, litigation funders are financing entire firms and their overhead across the US. A large percentage of BigLaw now takes some litigation funding (as do a fair percentage of younger and less successful litigation boutiques), and some firms have their entire litigation docket supported by litigation funders.

The very fact that a law firm takes funding reveals something about the strength of its business. For a law firm to allow a litigation finance firm to profit off of its work suggests that it is either desperate for the safety of the regular income or unwilling to take risks and bet on its own success. Or both. These are not signs of financial health. In the end, a firm's willingness to accept litigation funding rather than take the upside demonstrates poor financial health.

At a time when increasing competition has become perilous for BigLaw, and when new boutiques and spin-offs are on the rise, lenders help firms that probably should not be in business. It is a weird combination of a subsidy provided by a parasite.

That cannot be good for the legal industry in the long run.

CHAPTER 15

AI Is About to Change Everything

So MANY YOUNG LAW STUDENTS are pulled into BigLaw because they perceive it to be the "safe" choice. By their nature, lawyers are risk averse. And BigLaw promises several attractive things:

1. Guaranteed $225,000 annual starting salaries.

2. Job safety (which is an illusion, as we discussed).

3. A defined career path (which is true for almost none of them).

4. An added résumé builder (without experience this is also a mirage).

5. Important legal training on how to be a lawyer (not true).

Here's the thing: Each of these apparent "low-risk choices" are not low-risk at all. They all ignore the elephant in the room. Let me be blunt: *AI is about to destroy the BigLaw hourly fee model.*

Not ten years from now. Not "someday." It's happening already. For those of you entering law school, there's a good chance the BigLaw hiring machine will be sputtering by the time you graduate.

Most BigLaw firms still rely on the same tired economic structure they've used for decades, a bloated pyramid built on armies of junior associates billing time on repetitive tasks. That model has survived for one reason: Inefficiency is profitable under the BigLaw model. Time-consuming work has always been good for hourly fee service providers.

While current versions of generative AI tools like GPT-4 have their limitations, it is already a massive time-savings device. Tasks that previously took hundreds or thousands of hours can now be done in much less time.

In its current form, AI requires a lawyer to interact with it to iron out the kinks—but what it can accomplish in a fraction of an associate's time is astonishing. And it is only going to get smarter and better. It will *never* get dumber. Even the task of overseeing the AI will get easier.

In fact, leading scholars and industry analysts now say out loud what the partners know privately: *AI-assisted lawyers can perform routine legal tasks much faster.*

Think about that, and its implications for the current BigLaw model.

In a business that bills for time, AI is an unstoppable freight train of efficiency.

And remember, clients don't care about hours, they care about results.

What does that mean for you?

The work that lawyers do is about to become streamlined

Many of the time-consuming tasks that BigLaw has made boatloads of money on in the past will become simplified in the AI era.

Let's take the initial preparation of a lawsuit. Over the course of my career, I have seen teams of lawyers take weeks and months to synthesize information and produce a ready-to-be-filed lawsuit. Soon, lawyers will be able to upload a database to an artificial intelligence engine and a very polished first draft of a lawsuit will be available almost instantaneously. Of course, lawyers will need to review it, but the time savings will be enormous.

The defense firm that is hired to defend the lawsuit will plug it into their artificial intelligence engine and spit out a comprehensive first draft of a motion to dismiss and brief in support.

Up until now, discovery has been a long, drawn-out ordeal, which typically lasts a year or more in large cases. Discovery is a billing bonanza for hourly fee law firms who can put dozens of associates to work on discovery-related tasks and then send five lawyers to a deposition that a dozen of them spent weeks preparing for. Make no mistake ... in large cases, discovery can cost tens of millions of dollars.

Summary judgment practice, expert reports, pretrial motions, and everything else required to get a case ready for trial will be drafted and ready for a lawyer to review in a fraction of the time that it currently takes.

Will a lawyer need to interact with artificial intelligence and fine-tune its output for all of these tasks? Of course.

The question is not whether a lawyer will still need to be involved—the question is simply: Will the same number of lawyers be required for legal tasks in the future? Obviously not.

What will happen when discovery takes weeks or even days? What will happen when deposition preparation is done by AI and a lawyer can start with the AI-generated questions and follow up with additional questions? How many lawyers will these tasks take? Again, far fewer.

What about our courts? Our judiciary is overworked and underpaid. There are some courts where it can be difficult to get to trial in less than five years. But even the best courts struggle to decide motions and get cases ready for trial.

What will happen if a judge, using AI and a couple of law clerks, can decide motions in a fraction of the time? What if default scheduling orders routinely set cases for trial in six to nine months and leave only a short period of time for discovery? Obviously, this would make things way more efficient for everyone.

But it will absolutely wreck the current BigLaw model.

What does that legal world look like with the wide-scale adoption of artificial intelligence? Well . . . we're all about to find out. But I strongly believe my prediction will largely prove true. There will be far less demand for new lawyers. And many of the lawyers currently practicing law will need to retool.

As AI grows more powerful, will lawyers be needed in the future? Of course. But the question is: How many lawyers will be needed in the hyperefficient future? One thing I know for sure, trial lawyers will be really difficult to replace. Human creativity and ingenuity will still matter in the future. Whatever the future holds, it is best to be prepared for it.

THE DEATH OF THE BILLABLE HOUR

Very soon, the billable hour will no longer be the most profitable way to bill clients. If a firm can't bill time by the hour, it can't make money under its current model. As AI takes hold, BigLaw will have to adapt its model and abandon the billable hour. And when the hourly model ends, and inefficiency is no longer profitable, then why would BigLaw keep all of its people?

In other words, if BigLaw suddenly finds that inefficiency does not give it more billable hours and make it more revenue, but actually results in greater expense and lower profitability, then the current structure will end.

The BigLaw conveyor belt may keep delivering thousands of law grads, but soon BigLaw will not need or want them.

What happens then? The foundation crumbles. The number of law firm bankruptcies and industry consolidation will increase. For decades, the size of BigLaw firms has grown and more and more firms have been consolidating to form larger ones. I predict that this trend cannot continue. In fact, I think it will end badly for many of them.

Some law firm leaders are already seeing the writing on the wall. Some are scrambling to adapt. Others are pretending the storm isn't coming. But across the board, the pressure is building. AI is slashing the hours required to complete routine work, and under the billable-hour model, that means revenue disappears.

This all means that hourly fee law firms, both big and small, will migrate to alternative billing. The moment that happens, their inefficiency will no longer be profitable. When that day comes, the pyramid structure will transform into a wine bottle. In other words, if it can't make money on junior lawyers, it stops hiring them. If the number of senior lawyers required in the future are no longer necessary, their jobs will disappear too.

Now here's the irony—and maybe a silver lining. A lot of the work that AI is going to eat? It's the same work that junior lawyers hate. The stuff that grinds people down. The soul-sucking, copy-paste, red-line-every-damned-sentence misery that's designed to teach "discipline," but mostly fosters resentment.

A young lawyer's value will cease to be measured by how many hours she can grind out. It'll be measured by judgment, creativity, and strategy. In other words, everything BigLaw has spent decades training out of people.

But let's stop pretending there won't be a trail of wreckage behind this shift.

Law schools will get wrecked too

If BigLaw stops hiring junior lawyers because AI can do the grunt work faster and cheaper, then where are all these law students supposed to go? Where are all these law schools, especially the top ones that funnel hundreds of grads each year into BigLaw, going to place their next class?

This isn't just a BigLaw problem. It's also a law school problem. Law schools cannot continue to charge $80,000 a year in tuition and pretend everything's fine while the market for young lawyers evaporates.

The math won't work anymore. The pipeline will break down. Entry-level labor will no longer be needed in the quantities the system was built to produce. But yet, law schools seem totally unaware of this. Even if they wake up, however, don't expect them to fix it. The biggest victims will be the schools most heavily dependent upon the BigLaw conveyor belt.

Most law school administrators and faculty have never practiced law in any meaningful way. They've never managed a case, never pitched a client, never built a team. So they'll keep selling the dream of BigLaw and high starting salaries and they'll keep pushing students into a funnel that's closing off in real time.

BigLaw will survive and be highly profitable for the few that remain

Here's the punch line: BigLaw will survive, but the version that made a fortune off inefficiency won't. The old model with its endless hours, doc review marathons, and war rooms packed with overworked twenty-seven-year-olds is on its way out.

What replaces the current BigLaw model is still taking shape. Some firms will shift to flat fees or subscriptions. Others will automate their commodity work and charge for strategic oversight. But none of them will be able to keep doing what they've always done. That is, of course, not if they want to keep clients.

There will be some BigLaw winners. The BigLaw rainmakers who have their own clients will actually make more money. Clients will still want specialists to handle their problems. Real trial lawyers will still be in high demand. These people will all win in the AI era.

Unfortunately, the legions of lawyers who perform the majority of billing on major hourly fee work will become dispensable. Many of them will be forced to look for other jobs.

But for young lawyers, chasing a BigLaw job right now is precarious. It may look prestigious, but you're standing in the path of a storm that doesn't care what your résumé says. AI doesn't care if you went to Harvard. It just does the work. Really fast.

And it's only getting faster. And it's going to wipe out a lot of legal jobs.

CHATGPT ACED MY FINAL EXAM
IN MINUTES

You probably know that an AI passed the bar several years ago. In fact, it scored in the ninetieth percentile. Nevertheless, I remained skeptical about how well AI would actually reason on a legal challenge that was more complicated than a multiple-choice test.

So, I decided to see how well ChatGPT could do on the final exam in my UT Law class called Complex Financial Litigation.

My class is a case-study approach, using real-world cases that I have handled over the course of my career. It is modeled on the Harvard Business School approach, which uses real-world examples to teach students the practical application of law.

I teach litigation the way it actually happens: how real lawyers build cases, exercise judgment, and solve three-dimensional puzzles. It's not a traditional class. I have no textbook. And much of what I teach is well off the typical theory-based path of most law school classes.

The take-home, essay exam for my class requires students to synthesize a complicated, fifteen-page fact pattern. They are then asked to write six summaries of various causes of action and then write two 750-word essays on the best two claims.

I uploaded this year's exam to ChatGPT without any instructions and just asked it to act as my student and take the test. In less than a minute, it began drafting an answer that fully complied with my instructions. In a few minutes it completed the exam in full compliance with the instructions (something that a number of my students failed to do).

But it was not just the speed at which it executed the project, it was also the substance that impressed me. I would grade the Chat-GPT answer a B+. Meanwhile, my exam takes students four to six hours to complete. The AI was lightning-fast and fairly effective.

And this was the *public* version of ChatGPT. And yet, the AI passed. Not just competently, but impressively. This happened in this year's spring semester—*May 2025*.

Again, this is just the current, public version. What's coming will be even faster. Even smarter. Even more disruptive. If you're headed into the legal profession thinking you can count on a job—think again.

The "safe" jobs disappear
all the time

Long before the AI tidal wave, BigLaw had been less safe than it appeared. When the financial crisis hit in 2008, clients paused transactions and many lawyers were left fighting to find work. Most hourly fee lawyers could maintain their utilization only by padding their bills.

The same was true across the country. Many firms did not announce job reductions. Lawyers were simply fired after hours and their offices cleaned out. Other people only found out the next morning, when they saw the lawyer's name tag was missing from the office door. That ensured utilization stayed high. No one wanted to be the next associate to be "disappeared."

Just because a law firm is large, or has a famous name, or even appears hugely successful, there is no guarantee it will always be around.

Law firms, even the biggest ones, are far less financially stable than corporations because they lack retained earnings, outside investment, and long-term capital structure. Most firms distribute the vast majority of their profits to partners each year, which means they operate with very little cash cushion. They can't issue stock, raise equity capital, or take on investors because almost all states prohibit a nonlawyer from owning a law firm.

As a consequence, a law firm's entire business is built on that year's collections. And if revenue dips, they start cutting costs fast. That's why even seemingly successful firms can collapse in a matter of months, while corporations often have balance sheets that allow them to weather downturns, restructure, or refinance.

As proof of BigLaw fragility, since 2000 we've witnessed a whole series of law firm bankruptcies:

- **January 2003:** Brobeck, Phleger and Harrison grew huge during the technology boom of the 1990s, when it started to accept equity from newly established tech start-ups instead of payment. In the early 2000s it grew to 1,100 lawyers. The dot-com bubble burst, the value of tech stocks tumbled, and the firm went bust owing a load of debt to the bank. As a result, it dissolved in early 2003.

- **December 2008:** The New York firm Dreier, founded by Marc Dreier, recruited lawyers on high salaries and spent millions of dollars on art for the firm's offices. Dreier was the only equity partner of the 250-lawyer firm. All the management was concentrated solely within his control. He was a fraud who ran a Ponzi scheme that stole $740 million from clients. Dreier went to prison, the firm dissolved, and the attorneys lost their jobs.

- **December 2008:** Heller Ehrman, a large international law firm with over 730 lawyers across fifteen offices, suddenly closed after a number of senior rainmakers left in the fall of 2008. After their departure, Heller's bank foreclosed on their line of credit, which was the final nail in the coffin.

- **September 2009:** Thelen Reid & Priest merged with Brown Raysman in 2006. The combined firm was approximately 800 lawyers. While Thelen had an old-fashioned method of paying partners based on the firm's performance, Brown Raysman paid partners regardless of their performance. Thelen had a large outstanding debt in 2008, when a number of senior partners began to leave. Soon thereafter, the firm filed for bankruptcy.

- **January 2011:** Howrey was the first national antitrust firm in the 1950s, and by 2010 it had become an overseas firm with 700 attorneys worldwide and fifteen offices in the United States. It disappeared within two years as partners quit and it was unable to pay its debts. It too ended up in bankruptcy.

- **May 2012:** Dewey & LeBoeuf was a 1,000-lawyer firm with a multi-hundred-million-dollar amount of debt that they used to acquire lateral partners, who were supposed to be rainmakers. They hired these rainmakers on high, guaranteed salaries. But again and again these lateral hires failed to generate revenues matching their representations. The firm struggled under the bloated salary structure and the mountain of debt it took on to pay them. Not long after, it went under. A thousand lawyers got up in the morning and by the evening they were out of work—because their employers did not understand how to run a business.

What does this all mean for the future?

As of 2025, law school applications are at ten-year highs. Many of the applicants are attracted by the high salaries paid by BigLaw firms. But what will happen if many of the jobs they're chasing are disappearing?

The conveyor belt will keep moving, but it will lead to nowhere.

I'm not the first to suggest the possibility that the BigLaw gravy train may be screeching to a halt. Richard Susskind, Brian Tamanaha, Paul Campos, and Jordan Furlong have all warned for years that the BigLaw model is bloated and unsustainable. They are right. Their predictions aren't speculative anymore. They're happening in real time.

AI is going to take many of the BigLaw jobs that employ thousands of law grads.

What will happen to the 40,000 or so law school graduates who will graduate each year for the next three years? That's the billion-dollar question. Because if AI continues to absorb the work that used to justify BigLaw's prodigious hiring, then those graduates will be entering a market that no longer needs them.

Assuming that I am correct and many legal jobs will be replaced by AI in the future, then choosing a career path that accounts for an AI future is, of course, vitally important. From my vantage point, BigLaw is the most vulnerable legal business in the legal industry.

As a result, the next few years could lead to even more BigLaw bankruptcies. As technology accelerates the decline of the billable hour, firms that rely on inefficient staffing and time-based billing will find themselves increasingly outcompeted.

The next few years will be Darwinian. Frankly, BigLaw has long been overdue for some housecleaning. The firms with strong business models and solid client bases will survive in a new, "lean and mean" form.

The lesson is simple: There are no guarantees in BigLaw—not even size or prestige can protect you from BigLaw's structural fragility. The "safe" job you might be tempted to take could vanish overnight. That's why it's so important to be even more thoughtful about your career as we enter a technological age like none of us has ever seen.

At least one thing is clear to me. Trial boutiques with specialized practices and strong client bases will survive. A solid plaintiffs' litigation boutique with a strong book of business should do even better in the AI world. As for everyone else, I am not so sure.

PART 4:

WHAT I LEARNED FROM A CAREER FIGHTING BULLIES

CHAPTER 16

How a Judicial Clerkship Helped Me (and Why You Should Consider One)

I F YOU'RE UNCERTAIN ABOUT YOUR CAREER PATH, a judicial clerkship is one of the best ways to delay making a career decision, while you get to both learn about the legal profession through real-world cases and meet great people who can help you in the future.

If you already have a starting job picked out that you believe will set you on the path to where you want to be, then maybe a judicial clerkship is not necessary. But if you are dissatisfied with the job opportunities in front of you (e.g., you are headed toward BigLaw), then I would encourage you to find a judicial clerkship. Even if you know you're on the right path and have the ideal job to start your career, I still recommend that you consider a trial court clerkship.

Full disclosure, as you will see later in this chapter, I followed none of the advice that I am about to lay out regarding the type of clerkship you should consider.

I blindly played clerkship roulette by applying to over 100 circuit judges and taking the first job offer I got. That job was in Brownsville, Texas, where I clerked for Fifth Circuit Judge Reynaldo G. Garza, whom you will read about. But what follows in this chapter is the wisdom I have learned in the thirty-four years since I took the job to be Judge Garza's law clerk.

IF YOU WISH TO PURSUE A JUDICIAL CLERKSHIP, YOU MUST START THE APPLICATION PROCESS NO LATER THAN YOUR 2L YEAR

If you wish to pursue a judicial clerkship, *do not wait*—start early. Most judges take applications during your 2L year of law school, but like summer clerkships, the application process for judicial clerkships also appears to be creeping earlier and earlier.

It would probably be a good idea to start your due diligence on a judicial clerkship by the end of your 1L year. Of course, the things that judges like to see (e.g., good grades, Law Review, etc.) cannot be obtained prior to the end of your 1L year, but you can always supplement.

Pursuing a judicial clerkship allows you to delay the decision on a starting job until a year after you graduate

One of the great advantages to pursuing a judicial clerkship straight out of law school is that you can delay your decision on a starting job until the end of your judicial clerkship, putting the decision off until what becomes in effect late in your 4L year.

The pursuit of a one-year judicial clerkship extends your decision on a starting job from early in your 3L year of law school until late in your clerkship. You might think extending your decision window by eighteen months is not that significant, but trust me—it is a lot of time.

PURSUING A JUDICIAL CLERKSHIP ENABLES YOU TO SAMPLE OTHER POSTGRADUATE SUMMER CLERKSHIPS AFTER YOUR 3L YEAR

If you pursue a judicial clerkship after you graduate from law school, you can take advantage of an additional summer to work for one or two law firms. Unlike other 3L students, or worse, students who have graduated without a job, your clerkship will insulate you from the stigma that attaches to those other students. By clerking after you graduate and having the ability to sample additional summer clerkships, you can avoid the trap many BigLaw firms set—you can compare and contrast your experience at many more firms.

A TRIAL COURT CLERKSHIP WILL ENABLE YOU TO LEARN MUCH MORE ABOUT THE CAREER PATH FOR YOU

If you want to become a trial lawyer, clerking for a trial court judge is going to really help you on your path. Of course, most people view appellate clerkships as more prestigious than trial court clerkships. For starters, there are fewer appellate clerkships than trial court clerkships. But after three years of academia, another year of briefs and writing is not going to help you very much in learning new information, much less learning about trials and the actual practice of law.

Trial court clerkships expose you to the everyday practice of law. Most importantly, you will see trials. And, if your judge is at all a mentor, you will get a year's worth of wisdom from your judge as you watch other lawyers practice their craft.

How better to know whether you would like to become a trial lawyer than to watch other trial lawyers in court? It's becoming harder and harder to get trial experience of any kind. But the starting path to seeing if becoming a trial lawyer is for you is to watch other lawyers in court.

While there is no substitute for actually being in the trenches and trying a case yourself, a trial court clerkship is the next best thing.

Additionally, as a trial court clerk, you will see and experience numerous areas of the law (unless you strategically choose a court with narrow subject matter jurisdiction).

THINK ABOUT THE GEOGRAPHIC FACTOR: IS THIS COURT IN A LOCATION WHERE YOU WILL FIND YOURSELF IN YOUR CAREER?

The geography of your judge and the court you clerk for are important. If you plan to work in Texas, you should clerk for a judge in Texas. During your clerkship, you will meet various lawyers, see and work on cases, and ultimately get a sense for the landscape of the local bar.

These are all valuable to your ultimate career. If you clerk in Colorado because you like to ski, you will certainly enjoy your free time more, but it will not advance your career as much as a clerkship in a city that you plan to eventually practice law in.

Once you clerk for a judge, you will necessarily benefit by being in that judge's orbit. Just like the sun, the closer you live and work in relation to your judge, the more power your judge will have to help you. If your judge has been on the bench for a while, the judge's former clerks will become an important part of your network. Although it is not always the case, it is more likely that a judge's former clerks are also concentrated nearer that judge (for some of the same reasons that I am laying out in this chapter).

Regardless of whether you are able to tap into the judge's former clerks and make them part of your network, it is almost certainly the case that your judge's network will be concentrated in the vicinity of the judge you clerked for.

Think about that for a moment. If the judge has friends in private practice, at the local US Attorney's Office, or in other jobs that you might wish to pursue, your judge could be instrumental in helping you get those jobs. In contrast, how helpful could a New Mexico judge be in getting you a job in New York where your judge does not know anyone?

Bottom line, one of the keys to a successful legal career is building a network through your clerkship judge.

Think about the subject matter of the court: Is this court likely to have the types of cases that interest you?

Of course, federal district courts are courts of general subject matter jurisdiction. That means that in federal district court, you will work on both civil and criminal cases. And make no mistake, there's a big difference between courts on the border and courts in financial centers. Courts on the border can have a criminal docket that occupies as much as 90 percent of their docket.

If you want to be a civil trial lawyer, you may not get enough experience on civil cases as, say, a clerkship in New York City. Likewise, a clerkship in Washington, DC, will have a fair percentage of administrative law cases and other government-related litigation, whereas a clerkship in Dallas or Houston will have a fair percentage of commercial cases.

One court to consider, if you are interested in corporate governance or the law of equity, is the Delaware Chancery Court. If you want pure subject matter that is commercial in nature, there is almost no better court than the Delaware Chancery Court. And even if you do not wish to practice law in Delaware, it is one of the few jurisdictions where it is common to have lawyers from out of state regularly appear before the court. The only downside is that there are no jury trials in Delaware Chancery Court.

So, you need to do your homework and make sure that the court you clerk for will have at least some cases that fall into the subject matter that interests you.

DO YOUR HOMEWORK ON WHICH JUDGE WILL MENTOR YOU

Not all judges are good mentors. Some judges can be difficult to work for, others are even tyrants. The only way to truly know whether a particular judge is likely to be a good mentor, and whether your clerkship will prove valuable, is to speak with that judge's former law clerks.

And remember, if your goal is to build a network, you will be well served by connecting with the judge's former clerks.

I got lucky: My judge was an amazing mentor and his network of former clerks was very connected

One of the most important decisions I made in law school was applying for a federal clerkship during my 2L year. It meant taking a serious pay cut for my first year out of law school, but it paid enormous dividends. At the time, starting salaries for BigLaw associates in New York were around $81,000. A federal clerkship paid just $34,000. But I figured if I chased the money right out of school, I'd end up on a very different—and probably less fulfilling—career path.

A clerkship is the legal world's version of a Harvard MBA. For someone from a so-called "bar school" law school like St. John's, it's a chance to add serious weight to your résumé. St. John's may not have topped the rankings, but I loved it. I learned a ton of actual law, as opposed to arcane theory. It also made me scrappy and hungry. My thought was that the clerkship would give me pedigree to go with my grit.

I grew up in a lower-middle-class household; my mom was a nurse and my dad was a janitor and jack-of-all-trades who worked one hundred hours a week doing anything he could to make a buck. That meant I turned up in law school with a good work ethic. I paused my social life for the first semester so I could work my ass off. When I got my grades back, I had to look at them twice. I ended up second out of eighty-one students in my section.

St. John's was practical. It focused on the bar exam, not abstract theory. At some schools, Law Review is a credential. At St. John's, it also meant financial aid. If you made the Law Review, half your tuition was covered. If you became an Editor, tuition was free.

I got on Law Review in my 2L year, became an Editor in my 3L year, and ended up paying full tuition only for my first year, half for my second, and nothing for my third. Tuition was $11,000 a year. So, I paid only $16,500 total for my entire legal education. Meanwhile, I worked thirty-two hours a week as a security guard to cover living expenses. I did my homework on the job. That's what value looks like.

I applied for a clerkship without a full appreciation for the big picture. I also got lucky. I didn't fully understand the difference between trial courts and appellate courts. I just knew that circuit courts were considered more prestigious. There are fewer circuit judges than trial judges, which means fewer spots, and if you want to clerk for the US Supreme Court, you basically need to come through a circuit court first.

I wasn't aiming for the Supreme Court. I just wanted to learn about the law. So I sent out applications to 150 federal circuit judges who took clerks from schools other than Stanford, Harvard, and Yale. Among the judges I applied to were two Fifth Circuit judges named Garza—one older, one younger.

THE JOB INTERVIEW THAT CHANGED MY LIFE

During my 2L year at law school, I rented a room from an eccentric guy in Queens who was never home. I had a cordless phone (which was a somewhat modern invention at the time) but the battery had died. My landlord had an old 1920s-style phone on the kitchen wall that you had to pick up and speak into the microphone.

One morning, a few days after I had sent out my clerkship applications, the phone started ringing at about 7:20 a.m. I had been out drinking the night before, and I picked up the cordless phone and said hello, only to realize that the battery was dead. So, I went to the kitchen to use the old-fashioned 1920s phone.

A voice said, "Hello, this is Judge Garza calling."

It was somewhat bizarre talking to a federal judge for the first time in my life on this antiquated phone. It was also unexpected because it did not fit what was envisioned as the "normal" process. I would soon realize that when it came to Judge Garza, nothing would be the "normal" way.

When my friends got interviewed for a clerkship, a law clerk or secretary would invite them to the judge's chambers to meet with the law clerks for thirty or forty-five minutes, then the judge would meet with them for fifteen or twenty minutes. Yet, here I was talking directly to Judge Garza, who told me, "Bill, I'd like to have you down to my house this weekend. You can stay in the bishop's room." I said, "OK, Judge, that sounds great." He concluded the call by saying, "Once you have your travel plans, you call Olivia in my chambers and give her the details." We then hung up.

I went back to bed and slept off my hangover. I woke up thinking, *Was that call real? An entire weekend with a judge? I've never even been to Texas.* And I had no idea what staying in the "bishop's room" meant. To make matters worse, I didn't even know which Judge Garza I had spoken with. The voice on the phone sounded older, however, so I concluded that it was likely Judge Garza in Brownsville, who was seventy-eight, instead of the forty-six-year-old Judge Garza in San Antonio.

It was in fact the seventy-eight-year-old Judge Reynaldo G. Garza, who was not only a Fifth Circuit judge in Brownsville, Texas, but an icon in the Texas legal community.

Judge Garza was the first Mexican American federal judge in the United States. He was appointed by President Kennedy in April of 1961 and was personal friends with LBJ.

I called the chambers in Brownsville and spoke to Judge Garza's secretary, Olivia. I said, "I spoke to the judge this morning about coming down this weekend and I have a few questions. What airport do I fly into?" Olivia started to tell me, "You can fly into Harlingen Airport," but a voice in the background interrupted, "Put him through, put him through." There I was, talking to Judge Garza *again.*

I did not want to bother Judge Garza with my travel arrangements, but I said, "Where will I stay? Do I need a rental car?" He said, "Don't worry. I'll pick you up at the airport and you will stay with me." Then he asked, "What will you be wearing?" I had never been south of Washington, DC, other than a trip to Disneyland when I was nine years old, but it was March and it was chilly in New York, so I said, "I'll be in blue jeans and a black leather jacket." The judge again responded with one of his trademark quips: "Fine...fine."

The judge then said, "You come on Saturday and go home Monday. You can see my chambers and you can stay in the bishop's room." I said, "OK, Judge. How will I know what you look like?" He said, "Look at *Federal Reporter* 767 F second. There is a memoriam on the inside of the cover with my picture."

The *Federal Reporter* is a collection of circuit court opinions. When I found the book, I found the memoriam and there was a picture of Judge Garza with big, goofy ears reminiscent of the sportscaster Howard Cosell.

At that time, if you were a student, they issued American Express cards that included two $99 vouchers to fly on Continental Airlines. Each voucher let you book a round-trip ticket anywhere in the United States, so I booked a flight to Harlingen, Texas, via Houston using one of the $99 American Express vouchers.

When my buddies realized that I planned on wearing jeans and a black leather jacket to meet the judge, they said, "Are you insane? You can't show up to meet a federal judge in blue jeans and a black leather jacket."

Realizing that they were right, I put on the only suit I owned, and my only pair of nice shoes, and I flew to Harlingen, Texas, via Houston.

My travel plans were disrupted by a tropical storm in South Texas, which caused Harlingen Airport to close. I called the judge at home and said, "Judge, we have a problem. The Harlingen Airport is closed, so I'm stuck in Houston." He said, "Why don't you see if there are any flights to McAllen?"

There was a flight to McAllen one hour later but there was only one seat left and it was in business class. So Continental Airlines upgraded me and I found myself sitting next to a Gulf War veteran flying home to see his family. It was his first time in business class too.

When I got off the plane I spotted the judge, walked over, and introduced myself. He looked me up and down and said, "Well ... goddamn ... you're not wearing a black leather jacket." I said, "No, Judge. I thought it'd be more appropriate to wear a suit." He said, "Brownnoser." I thought, *I'm going to like this guy.*

It turned out everyone in the Rio Grande Valley in South Texas knew Judge Garza. Four or five people from the McAllen flight were also diverted like me and they queried, "Hey, Judge, could we hitch a ride back to Brownsville?" "Fine, fine," he told everyone. Then, he leaned over and said to me, "You sit in the front."

We all got in his 1983 Jeep Wagoneer with wood paneling and we drove slowly along the Rio Grande, along the Texas-Mexico border back to Brownsville. There was so much water on the road that a fifty-minute drive took over ninety minutes. The judge shocked me when he pointed at the river and said, "Goddamn . . . look at the *wetbacks* swimming across." He was the first Mexican American federal judge and by far the most prominent Hispanic person I had ever met, and he was using a racially charged term.

He went on to tell us all stories about JFK, LBJ, and the Cuban Missile Crisis. By the time we reached Brownsville in the middle of the afternoon, and dropped everyone off, the judge said, "Would you like to go to Mexico and have lunch with me?" I said, "Of course."

We drove across the bridge and had lunch at Garcia's, which is a famous lunch place in Matamoros. During lunch, the judge asked, "Would you like to drink some whiskey?" I hesitated. He said, "You drink whiskey, right?" I said, "Judge, I'm drinking whatever you're drinking." We ended up having three or four whiskeys.

At the end of lunch the judge said, "Well, it's a Saturday night in March, and I'm guessing you know what spring break is." I said, "I'm familiar with the concept." He said, "Well, I knew you wouldn't want to spend Saturday night with an old fart like me, so I've asked my law clerks to come pick you up, take you to spring break on South Padre Island, and bring you back tomorrow night. You'll stay in the bishop's room."

I said, "Judge, I keep hearing that name. What is the bishop's room?" He said, "Why . . . that's where the bishop stays when he comes to town."

Judge Garza was a Knight of Columbus who loved everything about the Catholic Church, so he had always wanted to hire a graduate of St. John's, which is a Catholic school. The judge also loved the fact that my dad had been a Trappist monk in the 1950s before he met my mom, who had been a Maryknoll nun. It was the one and only time in my life that my Catholic background came in handy.

The law clerks picked me up and took me out to South Padre Island, where we drank until 2:00 a.m. During the evening, they told me various Judge Garza stories and relayed how all of the other Fifth Circuit judges loved and respected him. At one point, I asked them, "Is this guy always like this? Drinking whiskey and telling stories?" They said, "Yep, that's him. Pretty much what you see is what you get." I thought, *OK, this is going to be pretty good.*

The next day, the judge and I watched the TV movie *Separate but Equal*, about the 1954 *Brown v. Board of Education* case. He told me stories about Thurgood Marshall, who argued the case in front of the US Supreme Court, and other Supreme Court justices, such as William O. Douglas, who was famous for the many wives he had over the years, all of whom were much younger than he was.

Judge Garza also told me how President Jimmy Carter had tried to offer him the position of attorney general in 1977. But Judge Garza told President Carter that he could not leave Brownsville, and thus, he could not accept the position as attorney general. Then, he told me how President Carter had called about a year later and said, "I want you to be a circuit judge. You turned me down once. You can't do it again." And, of course, the judge accepted.

On Monday morning we all sat down for breakfast. It was just Judge Garza, his wife Bertha, and me. I gave the judge a bottle of whiskey that I knew he liked to thank him for inviting me, and he called me a brownnoser again. It was clear that he liked me. For my part, I really liked him.

Toward the end of breakfast, he said while looking at his wife rather than me, "Bertha ...I'm thinking of making Bill an offer." I said, "Judge, I'm right here. Is that an offer or not?" Turning to me, he said, "Well, goddamn . . . I reckon it is."

I said, "Judge, I'm sure that there are better locations and better clerkships out there, but I'm a big believer in taking the bird in the hand over the two in the bush. So I'm going to take your offer—*but I have one request.*"

The judge paused, turned his head questioningly, and said, "A request? That's not how it works. What could you possibly request?" I replied, "Judge, your law clerks told me there is a party next month to mark your thirtieth anniversary as a judge." He looked at me curiously and remarked, "Why sure, why sure . . . there is."

I asked, "Could I please come to the party so I can get to meet all of your former clerks and gain a better understanding of what I just signed up for?" The judge leaned back and smiled and declared with his signature grin, "Well . . . no law clerk of mine has ever attended my anniversary party *before* they were my law clerk . . . *but goddamn, I don't see why not!*"

Judge Garza had been working for three decades, with two clerks every year—and every one of those sixty clerks came to his thirtieth anniversary party in April 1991. It was only appropriate because they were all part of the judge's extended family.

As someone who had grown up not knowing a single lawyer, I had (without realizing it) tapped into a network of successful lawyers who were all bound by my soon-to-be mentor. And not just average lawyers—sixty former federal law clerks, about half of whom were Fifth Circuit law clerks.

And they were all willing to help me on my career path. One of the clerks I met at the anniversary party (Ted Stevenson, a national trial lawyer in his own right) became a lifelong friend and another mentor in my career.

It might not be entirely true to say that my career would not have happened if I had not sought out a clerkship and then had the foresight to attend that party—but it certainly would've been more difficult. Again, it's often said that you make your own luck, but there is no denying that I hit the jackpot when I landed the Fifth Circuit clerkship with Judge Garza and joined his family of law clerks.

I eventually spent a year clerking for Judge Garza from 1992–1993 after I gained my JD. To this day my fellow Garza clerks remain like family. More to the point, until his death in 2003, Judge Garza was a constant and steady influence in my career.

During my clerkship with Judge Garza in Brownsville, I got to sit through a year of dinners and stories. I met all the judges and law clerks on the Fifth Circuit, which sits primarily in New Orleans but also in other places, including Austin. Everywhere, people came out in droves to meet Judge Garza. He was a superstar in that universe, even among the other Fifth Circuit judges.

The judge took me everywhere that year. I was able to attend every one of his sittings, which meant being away from Sunday to Thursday. He always gave me the civil cases, because he thought they were more complicated than criminal law, which was simpler and less interesting. I learned a ton.

Most clerks got to go out with their judge for dinner on one of those evenings out of the entire five-day sitting, but I went out with Judge Garza *every* night and on every sitting in the year I spent with him. That gave me access to a career's worth of legal wisdom over many meals and interactions.

CHAPTER 17:

Experience Beats Salary Early On

T HE MOST VALUABLE THING A YOUNG LAWYER CAN COLLECT isn't
dollars—it's experience. Especially if you want to be a trial lawyer, what
matters most early in your career is getting trials, not chasing paychecks. A
lower-paying job that puts you in a courtroom is worth far more than a high-paying
job that keeps you behind a desk. Trial experience not only makes you better, it gives
you options.

If you're going into law to be a hero, prepare for a rude awakening, especially if
you imagine the courtroom as your stage. The truth is, most "litigators" are paper
pushers who spend their careers avoiding court. Ninety-nine percent of civil cases
settle. Many "litigators" go their entire careers without ever seeing a jury box.

Dean Bobby Chesney at UT Law School tells a great story. The head of litigation
at his former BigLaw firm once told him, "If we're in a trial, we've made a mistake."
That's *exactly* how BigLaw sees it.

But if you want to be a trial lawyer, then you have to go to trial. In my experience,
a huge number of BigLaw "litigation partners" *have never tried a case.* They may be
brilliant brief writers. But they aren't trial lawyers. Trial lawyers are the lawyers who
actually go to court and try cases.

In several of my big cases, the BigLaw firm representing the defendant brought in an outside trial lawyer at the last minute. It's crazy, but many BigLaw teams I've faced *have never actually tried* a case. Clients with real litigation risk want someone who's been in the fight the same way someone who needs brain surgery doesn't want a theorist—they want a surgeon who's actually used the scalpel.

The problem is, *trial opportunities are disappearing*. In 1960, about 20 percent of federal civil cases went to trial. Today, that number is less than 0.5 percent. In criminal law, only 2 percent of federal cases and less than 3 percent of state cases go to trial. The right to a jury trial may be in the Constitution—but the jury trial itself is dying.

That means real courtroom experience is becoming increasingly rare. And if you want it, you have to go out and get it. That almost certainly means *not* starting your career in BigLaw.

No matter what kind of law you end up practicing—unless it's purely transactional—having trial experience will make you better. It will also give you more career flexibility. You'll learn how to think on your feet. How to read people. How to make judgment calls under pressure.

And if you're lucky, it might even make you love the law.

Because if you care about what you're doing—*if you actually want to make a difference*—then learning how to stand up in court and fight for something real might be the best decision you ever make.

How I learned from my miserable BigLaw 2L summer clerkship

Like almost everyone else, I was on the BigLaw conveyor belt during my 2L year. At St. John's, landing a BigLaw summer job basically required being near the top of your class and on Law Review. I had both, so before I ever got the offer from Judge Garza, I'd already locked in a summer clerkship with Rogers & Wells, a 400-lawyer firm in New York.

In 1991, I was making $1,185 a week as a summer clerk at Rogers & Wells. It was insane money at the time. I'd been earning that much per *month* as a security guard, working thirty-two hours a week. I thought, *This is going to be awesome.*

I was wrong.

When I got there, every last one of the thirty-five summer clerks in my class was miserable. Worse than that, so were the full-time associates. None of them had been to court or taken a deposition. Only partners could sign pleadings. There appeared to be no training at all. Alarm bells were soon ringing about the likely experience I would gain.

I shared a small office with a third-year transactional associate. On my second day, he was wearing the same tie I had complimented the day before. I said, "It's a nice tie, but why have you worn it for two days in a row?" He said, "I worked all last night and I'm still here. We went to the printer last night."

I learned later that "going to the printer" is what transactional lawyers call all-nighters when they prepare documents for big transactions such as mergers or IPOs. I also learned that I wanted no part of "going to the printer"—or of transaction law, whatever that was. I had no idea what "going to the printer" entailed, but it sounded miserable.

Then came the assignment that sealed it.

One day that summer, an associate in the banking department gave me a research project: figure out whether a foreign bank could legally send $500 million of its own money to its US affiliate. It seemed like it should be allowed. It was the bank's money, but there were complications.

For five days, I combed through the Code of Federal Regulations (CFR). In volume seven, section one, whatever-it-was, I found the provision covering this proposed transaction. Buried in that section was language that said in effect, "You can't do this. If you have any questions, call this number."

So I called the number thinking I would go the extra mile. A woman answered. I said, "I'm calling about CFR volume seven, section one, whatever-it-was. It says this transaction isn't allowed. Is there a way around that?" Without hesitation she asked, "Are you a summer clerk?" I said yes. She queried, "Where do you work?" I gave her the name of a different firm (this was before caller ID). She paused and said, "What you're describing is a felony. You might want to pass that along." I thought to myself, *Oh shit!*

I was still proud of finding the needle in the haystack, so I told the associate, "I found that CFR section." He said dismissively, "Oh yeah, we know about that." I asked him, "What do you mean? You sent me out to find what you already knew existed?" He condescendingly said, "Yeah."

I said, "Well, I called the number." He turned white as a ghost and blurted out, "You called Treasury?" He actually looked scared, and I started to feel sorry for him. I tried to defend myself and said, "I didn't know it was Treasury." All he could do was say, "You called the US Treasury?" I said, "It said to call if you had any questions." He said, "No one told you to call Treasury." I said, "I know. I was trying to go the extra mile in my research."

The associate looked at me derisively and ordered, "Take no further action on this matter." The way he concluded the conversation made me lose my sympathy for him.

Then he went and got another lawyer. They got another lawyer, and they all went into the partner's office and closed the door. No one came out for hours. No one asked me another question about the assignment.

Out of the thirty-five summer clerks at Rogers & Wells that summer, I was the only one not to get an offer. I am pretty sure that was the reason. And that was fine by me. I did not want to go there. The only time I'd done what I thought a lawyer did and combed through the law books until I found the point we needed, I got no praise. I'd only gotten myself into trouble.

That fall, I saw a report on *60 Minutes* about the Bank of Credit and Commerce International—BCCI. It turned out to be the largest financial fraud of the era, a tangle of cross-border scams involving billions of dollars, secret accounts, and Arab banking networks. BCCI was the client behind the CFR question I'd been asked to research.

The case went into liquidation in the Cayman Islands and dragged on for two decades. It's exactly the kind of complex financial fraud I go after today, which, in hindsight, is more than a little ironic.

That assignment was the final straw. I knew I could never work for a firm like Rogers & Wells.

Meanwhile, meeting Judge Garza's law clerks at his anniversary party that previous spring had changed my ambitions as a law student. A lot of Judge Garza's former clerks were older, and many were from the South, and they all encouraged me to try Texas.

So I started to seriously consider it.

Ted Stevenson, whom I'd met at Judge Garza's anniversary party, worked in Dallas and suggested I consider it as a place to launch my career. When I asked if associates actually got experience, he said, "I've been to court a ton in my four years." He'd even argued a case en banc before the Fifth Circuit—meaning he stood before every active judge on the court. That's rare for any lawyer, let alone an associate.

Other young lawyers from Texas told similar stories. They were taking depositions, going to hearings, even participating in trials. It was a stark contrast to what I'd seen in New York, where associates were buried in doc review and couldn't even sign pleadings.

Seeing young lawyers on the kind of path I wanted to be on convinced me: Dallas was where I'd like to start my career. That fall, during my 3L year, I started interviewing with Texas firms for post-graduation summer clerkships. By then, I'd completely given up on the idea of working in New York. I wasn't even planning to take the New York bar. Why bother sitting for a bar exam in a state in which I had no interest in practicing law?

My classmates at St. John's thought I'd lost my mind. "You went to a New York bar school and you're not even taking the bar?" they asked. "No," I said. "I'm clerking in Dallas next summer, before I clerk for Judge Garza."

The clerkship gave me an unexpected bonus: an extra summer to try out two different firms in Dallas. I accepted offers at both so I could see where I fit best. The difference between the Texas firms and Rogers & Wells was eye-opening.

First, young lawyers were actually making a difference. They were trusted with responsibility. They were going to court, taking depositions, and getting real litigation experience. No junior associate in New York was doing that.

Second, people stayed. Unlike in New York, where most young lawyers left after a few years burned out and disillusioned, associates at the Texas firms seemed not only invested, but also invested in. They had a real shot at making partner. The track wasn't a mirage. It was a possibility.

Both firms offered me jobs starting the following fall, after my clerkship with Judge Garza. I chose Hughes & Luce.

MY FIRST EXPOSURE TO TRIALS WAS DURING MY CLERKSHIP

My first exposure to a real trial happened during my clerkship for Judge Garza. One floor below our chambers, Judge Filemon Vela was presiding over a capital murder trial against Juan Raul Garza, a Mexican drug trafficker accused of multiple killings tied to a criminal enterprise.

When I was caught up on my work, I got permission to go watch. From the opening statements, I was hooked. I had never seen a live trial before. I kept sneaking down every chance I got. That courtroom and its energy lit something up in me. That trial made me want to be a federal prosecutor.

It was also my first look at how powerfully the law can collide with personal values. Judge Vela, a man who opposed capital punishment, sentenced Garza to death under the 1988 Anti-Drug Abuse Act, which was a law that allowed for the death penalty in drug-related murders. I still remember Judge Vela's remarks. He made clear that he didn't personally support the death penalty, but he felt bound by the law and the jury's findings.

That moment landed hard. It showed me the gravity of what judges and lawyers do and how it affects real people's lives.

Judge Vela also ran mock trials for local high school students. He invited me to join his law clerks and we "tried" made-up cases in front of him for the students. Judge Vela presided over mock trials in which the law clerks acted as trial lawyers, actual federal agents were witnesses, and various students were selected to serve on the jury. The goal was to ensure that the drug defendant was convicted and sentenced to a lengthy sentence.

It was the first time I ever stood up in a federal court and made an argument, even if it wasn't "real." That experience, combined with watching the Garza trial, cemented something in me: I wanted to be in the courtroom. I was going to be a trial lawyer. It still took me a while to get there, but that seed was planted in Brownsville.

One of the highlights of my clerkship was "afternoon coffee" with Judge Garza and Judge Vela. Every day at 3 p.m., the judges and clerks would gather to drink coffee and swap stories—usually about trials. They'd tell war stories, joke, reflect. We also played a quarter game where the judges picked a number between 1 and 499, and the clerks had to guess it with only "higher" or "lower" clues. Winner took the pot. But no one came for the quarters. We came to soak up the wisdom—and the stories. And almost all of those stories came from the courtroom.

I ENJOYED HUGHES & LUCE, BUT IT WASN'T ENOUGH

After finishing my clerkship with Judge Garza, I took my $5,000 signing bonus, maxed out my credit cards, and took off. I backpacked through Mexico, enrolled in a language school to improve my Spanish, and spent every last dollar. Then I came back to Dallas, Texas, and launched my legal career.

My first real job was at Hughes & Luce in Dallas. It turned out to be a smart choice. The firm had a strong trial practice and, unlike most BigLaw firms, it handled both plaintiffs' and defense work. That gave me a valuable early perspective: I got to see litigation from both sides.

It also gave me something else. Real opportunities.

My mentor, Ted Stevenson, advised me to take over the landlord-tenant docket. He said it would get me into court fast. And he was right. Cheryl Lasseter, the senior paralegal who ran the docket, made sure I got my reps. I handled motions, argued hearings, and tried cases. They weren't glamorous, but they were mine. And early in your career, nothing is more important than getting in the game.

The firm also gave me a window into international work. I got to travel to Peru, Mexico, and even Beijing, China. I got real experience that allowed me to take on responsibility and see the world. Hughes & Luce offered me a broad education, domestic and international, plaintiff and defense.

I also got to take depositions, argue in court, and second-chair larger cases. But on the big-ticket trials, I was still third chair. I didn't want to be close to the action—*I wanted to be the action.*

One of the firm's stars was Bob Mow, a top trial lawyer in Dallas. When a case really mattered—plaintiff or defense—Bob was the guy people called. I didn't want to be just a trial lawyer. I wanted to be the kind of lawyer Bob Mow was—the go-to trial lawyer.

And I realized the only way to become one was to get deeper, faster trial experience as a lead.

So, in the spring of 1997, I told the firm I was leaving to join the US Attorney's Office as a federal prosecutor.

I made an economic sacrifice to get experience, as I did when I took my judicial clerkship. Joining the government as an assistant United States attorney at the age of twenty-nine, my salary was roughly one-half of what I was making in private practice. My dad could not understand my decision. Nor could Judge Garza. They both questioned what I was doing, but I realized trial experience was the key to unlocking the career I wanted, so I needed to work for the government in order to get that experience.

A Goodbye Lunch with the Proverbial Harvard Law Grad

The news of my departure surprised many of my colleagues at Hughes & Luce. Shortly after I announced it, I was invited to lunch by Eric, the chair of the litigation department. Eric was a Harvard Law grad. Over lunch, he told me, in so many words, "You'll get tired of being a prosecutor. When you're ready to come back, there'll be a spot for you here."

It was a generous offer, and I appreciated it. But toward the end of our lunch, Eric said something that revealed just how rigid some lawyers can be in their thinking. He asked, "How can we attract more lawyers like you from Columbia?" I didn't miss a beat. "Eric, I went to St. John's." He didn't blink. "You know what I mean . . . from the Northeast."

I was flabbergasted. I couldn't tell whether he was unintentionally flattering me by assuming I went to Columbia or unintentionally insulting me. One way or another, his statement reflected the arrogant notion that a good lawyer must have gone to an elite law school (like Eric who, incidentally, quit practicing law soon afterward to write sci-fi novels).

Here's the truth: If you didn't go to an elite law school, someone will judge you for it. At some point, someone will assume you're less capable because of where you went to school. It's a built-in bias of the profession.

But it's also completely wrong. And most of the arrogant people who hold those views are the same people who are forced to trade on their academic résumé because they failed to achieve much during their actual career.

The bottom line is that I am living proof that it matters much more *what you do with your career* than where you got your diploma. And I am proud that I went to St John's. I got a great education steeped in practical knowledge.

Three years as an AUSA made me a
Trial Lawyer

Despite Eric's polite "warning," I left Hughes & Luce after four years and became an assistant United States attorney (AUSA) in Del Rio, Texas. And I never looked back.

Del Rio is, frankly, a godforsaken town. About 150 miles west of San Antonio, right on the Mexican border, it had a federal air base, two restaurants (both terrible), and a stretch of the Rio Grande so shallow you could wade across it. That geography made it a frontline post in the drug war and gave it one of the largest criminal dockets in the country.

From the day I arrived, I told everyone I was there for three years, no more. They all said the same thing: "You're crazy. No one takes this job for just three years." I said, "We'll see."

In the Northeast, the prestige path runs from an elite law school to a federal clerkship to the US Attorney's Office. Plenty of AUSAs show up with zero trial experience.

In the South, it's the reverse. Most AUSAs come up through the District Attorney's Office. They've already tried dozens of state-level cases before moving to federal court, which is seen as more prestigious and higher paying, even if it offers less raw trial action.

I didn't follow either track. But by going to Del Rio, I gave myself something rare: real volume, real courtroom time, real autonomy. In just three years, I became what most litigators never become: *a real trial lawyer.*

At twenty-nine, I was by far the youngest prosecutor in the office—and one of the youngest in the entire district. I had tried to land AUSA jobs in other districts, but they all turned me down. The reason was always the same: I didn't have enough trial experience. Which, of course, was the exact reason I wanted the job in the first place.

And I got what I came for: trials.

In those three years, I tried twenty-five jury trials. Some prosecutors do eight-year stints and never get that many. But I was single, had nothing to do but work, and I hunted for trial time. There were seven AUSAs in our office. Everyone else was married with families. I didn't have much to distract me, so I threw myself into the work.

I AGGRESSIVELY SOUGHT TRIAL EXPERIENCE AS AN AUSA

Every month we'd have docket call before the district judges to determine the order of the jury trials set for the following Monday. I'd lobby my fellow prosecutors for any of their cases that were set ahead of mine so I could get more trial experience.

Whenever I could, I'd try to get the case moved out of Del Rio. The trick was convincing the judge, usually visiting from San Antonio, that the trial would take more than two days. That was the magic phrase. No judge wanted to stay in Del Rio for more than two days. So, if you said "three or four days," the case got moved to San Antonio.

In the end, I tried all but a few of my jury trials in San Antonio. It was my unofficial ticket out of Del Rio.

ONE OF MY ADVERSARIES BECAME AN UNLIKELY MENTOR

I had friends in the Del Rio US Attorney's Office. In fact, Mark Patterson, the lead prosecutor in the Juan Raul Garza case, which was the very trial that inspired me to become an AUSA, was in the office. But as for mentorship? I was largely on my own. No one in that office was able to fill that role.

Fortunately, I found mentorship in an unlikely place: on the other side of the courtroom.

Alan Brown was a well-known criminal defense lawyer in San Antonio. I'd met him years earlier when I dated his daughter, but we reconnected while I was stationed in Del Rio. He had clients down there and came in regularly. When I was in San Antonio for trials, I'd see him there too.

We talked shop, swapped stories, and over time, Alan became a major influence on how I viewed the profession and how I wanted to practice law.

Alan was quiet in public, almost reserved. But in the courtroom, he was magnetic. He'd won dozens of murder trials, mostly on self-defense grounds. His success rate was so high it made federal prosecutors nervous. Some of my colleagues couldn't believe I spent time with him.

"Wait—you're friends with *that defense lawyer*?"

Yes. I was. But more importantly, he was a hell of a trial lawyer. I took him to dinner whenever I could. I picked his brain. And I made sure never to go easy on his clients because I wasn't about to give anyone any excuse to question my integrity.

Alan was one of the first real trial lawyers I got to know up close. He talked about cases constantly. He'd bounce ideas off waiters, bartenders, anyone who'd listen. He wanted to know how regular people reacted, because those were the people who ended up in the jury box. If something landed, he'd use it in court. That was one of his superpowers: reading people.

I still use some of his strategies today.

During that same stretch, I also learned a lot from Judge Fred Biery. We shared more than a few forgettable meals in Del Rio, but the conversations and the wisdom he conveyed to me were invaluable. Over dinner, he'd encourage me to try winging it more in court, to trust myself, to stop leaning on outlines. He was right. I performed better without notes. Still do.

In my experience, judges tend to be more willing to spend time with government lawyers than with private ones. So it wasn't unusual for a prosecutor to go to dinner with a judge, but it was unusual to go to dinner with a defense lawyer. I did not care.

Being an AUSA confirmed I really wanted to be a trial lawyer

Between Alan, Judge Biery, and my time as an AUSA, I didn't just rack up trial experience, I started to figure out who I was as a lawyer.

And what I discovered was this: *I loved being in the courtroom.*

There's nothing else like it. The adrenaline. The focus. The clarity of purpose. Trial work gave me a sense of alignment I'd never felt anywhere else. Even if I was getting only four hours of sleep, even if I was waking up at 3 a.m. with my mind racing, it was worth it. It is still invigorating.

But I also knew this: I didn't want to be a criminal defense lawyer like Alan. The criminal trenches are noble, but relentless. Day in, day out, year after year, it wears you down.

And I didn't want to stay a prosecutor either.

The criminal justice system takes a toll on everyone involved. During my time as a federal prosecutor, I often felt empty after winning.

Winning didn't feel like winning.

A "successful" prosecution usually meant sentencing someone to decades in prison. I'd sit in court and watch twelve or fifteen young men get hammered with long, mandatory sentences and I'd walk out feeling … nothing. Or worse—depressed.

There was no satisfaction in that. No sense of justice served. Just a gnawing feeling that I was part of a machine. I knew I couldn't make a career out of that. I didn't want to spend my life meting out punishment. I wanted to fight for something that I found more meaningful. I wanted to win battles that mattered to me, and win them on my own terms.

That's when it became clear: ***I wanted to go after wrongdoers, not just drug traffickers.***

I wanted to use the courtroom as a weapon for accountability, not just punishment. I wanted to take the skills I'd learned and aim them at people who abused power, broke trust, and thought they could get away with it.

That's when plaintiffs' law started to make sense.

I'd been thinking about what to do with my career all along, of course. It was Alan who first told me, "Bill, if you want to be a trial lawyer, you should be a plaintiffs' lawyer. It's way more fun than criminal law, and it's where the real money is."

No one had ever put it that clearly for me before, and although it did not immediately register, eventually it clicked—when luck struck.

CHAPTER 18:

My New Career as a Plaintiffs' Lawyer

T HE SEEDS OF REID COLLINS were sown while I clerked for Judge Garza, who was himself a former plaintiffs' lawyer. During my clerkship in 1992–1993, he had two sittings on the Fifth Circuit in Austin, Texas. From the moment I arrived, I was drawn to Austin's energy. I remember thinking: *I have to live here someday.*

Eight years later, I got my chance.

In March 2000, as I was starting to look beyond my AUSA job, my good friend (and fellow Garza clerk) Ted Stevenson called. He told me that a group of my former colleagues from Hughes & Luce had just announced they were leaving to launch a plaintiffs' firm. Their focus? "Who Killed the Company?" cases—complex commercial fraud, corporate collapse, and high-stakes litigation. Eight of them had broken away and started a firm with offices in Dallas, Houston . . . and Austin.

I immediately seized the opportunity. Soon thereafter, I reached out and they offered me an associate position.

On June 1, 2000, I left the US Attorney's Office in Del Rio, three years to the day. I'd always been interested in plaintiffs' work, even in law school and during my clerkship, but I had no clear path into it. Honestly, I didn't even know what kind of plaintiffs' law I wanted to practice. But now all of a sudden the most ideal practice I could imagine just landed in my lap.

Joining a plaintiffs' firm in Austin, Texas

Becoming a plaintiffs' lawyer in Austin felt like an idiot test. It was an easy decision. I became the firm's ninth lawyer, and several of my partners today are fellow Diamond McCarthy alumni.

Although I came in with more trial experience than anyone else, thanks to twenty-five criminal trials as a federal prosecutor, I was hired as an associate. The firm, like so many others, operated on a lockstep model, which rewarded seniority over skill.

I started to resent the lockstep approach. It became clear to me that a meritocracy, where contributions were more important than seniority, was far superior.

Still, I stayed focused on the long-term upside. I was thirty-two, and while Austin wasn't exactly a hotbed for high-end plaintiffs' work, it was where I wanted to live. And that mattered. I bet that I could build a career around the life I wanted, not the other way around.

That's harder to do in the billable-hour world. Hourly fee lawyers are, in many ways, geographically bound. Since they're largely interchangeable, geography becomes part of the pitch. But when you do plaintiffs' work—especially commercial trial work on a success fee basis—you're selling expertise, not proximity. I didn't need to be near the client. I needed to be able to win.

So that's what I built: a niche that had real demand and could be sold from anywhere, including Austin, even though I've had very few significant cases based in Austin since moving there in 2000.

If you're thinking about where to live and practice, here's my advice: choose geography based on where you'll thrive as a human being, not just where the work happens to be. With the rise of pro hac vice admissions and remote practice—especially post-pandemic—location matters less than ever. And if you focus on developing rare, in-demand skills, you'll have the leverage to live wherever you want.

My first day of work brought me to the Cayman Islands

On my first day of work as a plaintiffs' lawyer in June 2000, I flew to the Cayman Islands for the civil side of a massive Ponzi scheme case being prosecuted by my former office, the US Attorney's Office in the Western District of Texas. Because there were legal proceedings in both the Cayman Islands and the US, I was able to experience my first multi-jurisdictional, cross-border fraud case.

A criminal named Jose Zollino, head of InverWorld, had been charged in the US with investment fraud (and would eventually be sentenced to twelve years in prison for orchestrating a $325 million Ponzi scheme). A liquidator was appointed in Cayman to oversee the Cayman entities, and a US bankruptcy trustee was appointed over the US entities.

The liquidator and the bankruptcy trustee were tasked with pursuing claims against, among others, lawyers and accountants. My primary job was to prosecute a claim against the accounting firm Deloitte for screwing up their InverWorld audits.

The Deloitte case lasted five years. I ended up settling it for $26.7 million. I was in my mid-thirties and it was by far my biggest settlement. It was my first experience of complex financial fraud on a success fee basis, and it was sexy as hell. The combination of solving the multidimensional chess board, winning the case, and collecting a sizable contingency fee was intoxicating.

It set me on the path to where I am today.

Among the other litigation claims available to the liquidator and trustee was a legal malpractice claim against the New York–based law firm Curtis Mallet-Prevost. The case settled relatively quickly and added to the firm's early list of calling cards.

I did not realize it then, but suing law firms was soon to become a niche practice.

The reason we started doing more and more legal malpractice claims back then was because no one else was doing them. People were afraid of suing other lawyers. The Curtis Mallet case was a big reason why potential clients began calling my firm to pursue other legal malpractice claims.

It was frankly another stroke of luck.

AFTER MY RETURN TO PRIVATE PRACTICE, I MET ANOTHER IMPORTANT MENTOR: DON NICHOLS

Soon after returning to private practice, my good friend Ted Stevenson introduced me to Don Nichols. Don quickly became one of my most important mentors. He would fundamentally change how I approached trial work. Don isn't a lawyer. He's a PhD in communications. But he's seen more trials than just about anyone I know.

I first worked with Don on a small bad-faith insurance case. The pre-suit offer was $300,000. After a three-week trial, we walked away with a $7 million verdict, which at the time was one of the largest ever in Travis County, Texas. Don was instrumental in that result.

I was hooked on Don. Since then, I've never gone to trial without Don. He's now in his eighties, and still, every time I gear up for a jury trial, he's there. And I haven't lost a jury trial since I left the government thanks to Don.

Don joins a small but critical list of people who helped shape my path—Judge Garza, Ted Stevenson, Alan Brown, and Don Nichols. All very different. None of them expected me to be just like them. But each one gave me something essential.

I cannot emphasize enough how important my mentors have been to my successful legal career. Mentors are essential for any lawyer trying to find the course to a career that will make them happy.

Our former firm's business practices forced our departure

Within a few years, in spite of my age I had risen to become the second-highest compensated equity partner at my former firm. How did that happen so quickly?

I was able to rise through the partnership ranks because my team and I were able to originate significant amounts of business. Like I told you earlier in the origination chapter, the lawyers who have the clients run the firm.

But I didn't like the way the firm ran its business. The firm's overhead was bloated. It spent a lot of money on expensive leases and made other extravagant decisions that provided no return to the business, but just sapped the firm's profitability.

The firm mainly stuck to less risky, hourly fee work that was not exciting, but paid the bills. Perhaps the biggest flaw with the business was that firm management borrowed money to pay the equity partners their regular draws, even when profits were not being earned. They were good lawyers, but I was struggling to see a future there for me or my team with their flawed business model.

Things came to a head when my wife was pregnant with our third child. We had two other children in diapers and my dad was terminally ill. The partners asked me to sign a guarantee to support an increase in the firm's line of credit from $5 million to $10 million. The partners' personal guarantees on the law firm debt were directly correlated to our partnership interest in the firm. Because I was the second-highest equity partner, I would have to guarantee the second-greatest proportion of the $10 million line of credit.

As the firm became reliant on using the line of credit to pay partner draws, its financial stability weakened. I knew this was a slippery slope and a recipe for disaster. I told the firm's management that I refused to continue to borrow money to pay partner draws. Draws should be funded only with firm profits—that's the way it is supposed to work. I could not and would not agree to borrowing additional capital to pay partner draws. I added that my team was the most productive in the firm, and if our future was imperiled by these unwise loans, then we were all out of there.

They told me, "Who the fuck do you think you are? Sign the note."

When I refused, they kicked me out. And my team followed me.

CHAPTER 19:

How We Formed a National Plaintiffs' Boutique

O N NOVEMBER 23, 2009, with little time to plan and even less certainty, Lisa Tsai, Jason Collins, and I, along with five other lawyers, launched our own plaintiffs' law firm in Austin, Texas. We had no active matters, no guaranteed clients, and very little cushion. Lisa and Jason were just thirty-two, and I was about a decade older.

We had a strong track record, we were self-sufficient as a team, and we'd been generating positive results for years.

But that didn't mean we were guaranteed to make it on our own. We weren't certain that our prior success would follow us. We weren't sure how vital the platform of a bigger firm was to our success. And we were worried about whether our vision of a plaintiffs-only, success fee-focused litigation boutique based in Austin, Texas, could succeed.

Still, we took the leap and bet on ourselves.

Meanwhile, at the old firm, we had just recruited a group of junior associates a year out of UT Law School. Our young recruits included Nate Palmer, who was second in his class, and Josh Bruckerhoff, who was not far behind. They had both made Law

Review and they were outstanding young lawyers. We wanted to take both of them with us, but our fiduciary duty to our old partners meant that we could not recruit them while we were still partners at our former firm.

Hours after we announced our departure and hastily formed Reid Collins, I got a call from Nate Palmer. Someone had told him that Lisa, Jason, and I had left to form a new firm and, understandably, he was upset that we had done so without even telling him. I was in New York City, trying to drum up new business, and I promised that when I got back to Texas at midnight that evening I would drive straight to his home and explain everything.

When I landed around midnight, I drove straight to Nate's house and sat down with him and his wife. I explained that it would've been a breach of fiduciary duty to my former partners to recruit anyone to join a new firm while I remained a partner at my old firm. I then laid out our plans for Reid Collins with them until 2:00 a.m., and Nate then decided to join our new firm.

Meanwhile, Josh Bruckerhoff was backpacking in Peru, where he was visiting Machu Picchu. I got a message to him that I would like to speak and he called me from a pay phone in Cuzco. He did not take much convincing to come with us too.

Nate and Josh were the two young associates that we started Reid Collins with in 2009. They could have gone anywhere but they took the even greater risk to come with us in a start-up law firm. I hope they feel it has paid off.

Both of them took a risk coming with us, and both are now equity partners at the firm. Looking back, that kind of loyalty and belief in our mission helped shape the culture of Reid Collins.

Reid Collins had an inauspicious start

From day one, we made two cardinal decisions that shaped everything:

1. The equity partners would not take home a dollar unless all bills were paid and the firm had enough cash to fund operations at least a month in advance, and,
2. We would *never* take on debt. *Ever.*

That meant that unlike many other firms, we were going to pay ourselves only true profits and we were going to leave cash in the firm.

At the time, our monthly overhead spend was less than $75,000 per month (today it is a lot more than that). It takes discipline to run a firm so leanly, but we have always been able to abide by these two rules.

In order to ensure that we had staying power, we limited all expenses of the firm. Beyond salaries for our lawyers, our first office lease was less than $10,000 per month. It was so dismal, we could hear rats running in the ceiling. We did not even bother with regular furniture—several of our lawyers worked on makeshift tables with cardboard boxes as legs. In essence, we ran the firm on a shoestring budget.

Personally, it was not the easiest time to start a new firm. My dad was terminally ill and lived the last month of his life in our home and passed away peacefully on January 14, 2010. In March of that year, our third child arrived, at which point we had three kids under three years old.

But we had a focused business plan to seek out success fee opportunities rather than hourly cases. This was particularly strategic in gathering business, because fewer lawyers are willing to take on that degree of risk. In other words, we faced less competition.

But it was also riskier—*a lot riskier.* Getting a pure alternative fee practice off the ground was not going to be easy until our docket produced results. In the meantime, we'd be left to fund our operations. Where our old firm had avoided risk but had been financially fragile, we were comfortable with risk, and used our risk tolerance to build the foundation of a stable business.

Luckily, we made a small contingency fee of about $1 million in January and another $2 million, April, 2010. And then we hit pay dirt.

In October of 2010, we made our first large contingency fee. That fee allowed us to give a bonus to everyone in the firm and ensured that we had staying power for months to come. And, as they say, the rest is history.

The first thing we did with our newfound success was to upgrade our office space. In May of 2010, we moved into the office space of a real estate firm that had left behind all of its furniture. It was not prime space, but at least we got away from the rat-infested dump we started in and now we had real furniture.

For the first seven or eight years, we gained success with cases that were more difficult than the ones we are able to get today. We have built a substantial national reputation by consistently winning cases other law firms turned down. And we carefully and thoughtfully added to our team over the years.

But the key was concentrating our docket on the sorts of things most law firms were reluctant to do. And we do it all on a success-fee basis, which gives us a massive competitive advantage.

Just a few of the things that make our firm different

Not many plaintiffs' boutiques are as pure plaintiffs' law as you might think. Many of the firms that you think of when it comes to plaintiffs' law still do a fair amount of defense work to pay the bills. Others even do hourly plaintiffs' work.

At Reid Collins, we are about as pure a success fee plaintiffs' firm as you'll find. There's one main reason for that: *Plaintiffs' work is more fun.*

Additionally, in order to take on an hourly fee case at our firm, you need approval from the intake committee, because our ethos is embodied in the excitement of contingent fee litigation.

One of the core strengths to our business model is that we have several niche practices that are in great demand. Our strongest niche is legal malpractice. We are willing to sue other lawyers, including the largest and most powerful law firms in the world.

But we also have a great deal of market power on plaintiffs' side, insolvency-related litigation. This is the part of our practice where we represent professional plaintiffs, like bankruptcy trustees and offshore liquidators.

Of course, we also do general complex financial litigation as well. But it helps to have national calling cards because many people can and will do complex financial litigation.

Here's how we think about it: Reid Collins operates like a hedge fund. But instead of investing cash like a traditional hedge fund, we invest human capital in the form of our time. Like a hedge fund making an investment, we do rigorous due diligence before taking a case. We assess risk, value, liability, collectability, and the opposition. We don't chase volume. We pursue high-value opportunities where we believe the investment of our time, skill, and strategy will generate a real return for us and our client.

Bottom line: At Reid Collins, we don't just sell legal services. We invest in our clients and in our cases. Our fee structures reflect that. We take on real risk because that's what lets us share in real rewards. And frankly, it makes it way more fun.

OUR COLLABORATIVE APPROACH TO MANAGING CASES

The main difference between our firm and BigLaw in terms of young lawyers is that we do not commoditize our associates. They are intimately involved in our cases, doing real work from the ground up and from the beginning. And because we are not incentivized to stack hourly billers on our cases, we give meaningful responsibility to all of our team members because unlike BigLaw, *being efficient is profitable for us.*

Even better, when we're in trial we have a policy to get everyone, even first-year associates, on their feet and give them witnesses to examine. The look of envy on the other side's demoralized associates who have no responsibility when they see our young people putting on witnesses is always satisfying.

That means that on our team even junior associates get meaningful experience from day one. Instead of ramping up our hours by having associates search through millions of pages of nonsense with the goal of billing more hours, we crave efficiency. As a result, we are incentivized to train our people from day one.

One of the benefits of having our own law firm is that it allows everyone to escape the tyranny of minimum hours. Our lawyers do not even fill out time sheets, so we cannot track our associates' hours. We pride ourselves on not asking people how many hours they are billing.

Instead, we focus on the substantive contributions that our lawyers make to each of our cases. We give them responsibility and expect them to do the work that is needed, ignore the work that is unnecessary, and help us achieve the goal of winning the case. Because the focus is on the result and the quality rather than the quantity of their work, our team ends up feeling more rewarded for making an actual difference in a case.

WE SUE AS A LAST RESORT AND PRIORITIZE A BUSINESS DISCUSSION

We learned that the first thing to do in a case is to send our adversaries a draft complaint along with an invitation to have a business discussion. Our clients do not want to go to court; they just want a result. Other law firms also do this, but we are unique in doing it in virtually every case as a matter of standard operating practice.

This pre-suit business discussion approach is particularly effective when a case involves disclosing embarrassing material and firing what we call a "one-shot gun."

Frequently, our adversaries are happy to resolve litigation and keep the genie in the bottle. If we were to file suit first, we've already shot our only bullet and then the defendant has nothing further to lose in fighting.

To elaborate, during our pre-suit approach we ask the other side if they want to know about our case. We offer a ready-to-be-filed lawsuit in exchange for a standstill agreement. Some lawyers see revealing your hand too early as a sign of weakness. I disagree. Why wait for some arbitrary event that might prompt a business discussion when we can foster a business discussion more efficiently? In effect, we give the defendant the choice as to whether it would like to be sued or not.

Sometimes the other side tells us to go jump in a lake, other times we spend a great deal of time and fail to agree on terms to resolve the case. But we still find that there is value in the pre-suit phase even when we fail to reach resolution, because we learn how to focus the case on what matters and to address any flaws identified by our adversaries during the pre-suit phase.

After fifteen years, other lawyers know that our firm is more than willing to file suit and, more importantly, proceed to trial if we cannot get a case resolved on terms satisfactory to our client. As a result, most of our adversaries take our offer of a pre-suit discussion very seriously. And if we sense that the other side has concluded that we are weak, then we're more than ready to stop playing Secretary of State and start playing Commander in Chief and go to war.

Far from being a sign of weakness, our standard operating practice of pursuing a pre-suit business dialogue in every case allows us to have a caseload twice as large as another firm of our size. This is because at any one time about 50 percent of our docket is at some stage of this pre-suit, business discussion, which is less labor-intensive, more efficient, and far more likely to achieve a result.

When our cases settle in the pre-suit, business discussion phase, they frequently involve a lot of premium dollars. In other words, we make more money on a pre-suit resolution, even at a lower success fee percentage, relative to the time that we invest in those cases. This is because we can better leverage our time in the pre-suit phase than the far more labor-intensive litigation phase.

When they do not settle, both sides know far more about what lies ahead, making any litigation more efficient.

How compensation works in my firm
versus other firms

Just like BigLaw, we pay our starting associates the same base pay of $225,000 per year. In fact, many other top-tier plaintiffs' firms pay a BigLaw starting salary. And at each rung of the ladder, we pay a competitive salary similar to what BigLaw pays.

But how and when firms pay bonuses, and how transparent they are about their finances, are more telling of a firm's philosophy.

Every December, one of the prominent BigLaw firms (historically Cravath) will announce its year-end bonus and issue a press release. Over the following weeks, BigLaw firm after BigLaw firm will announce that they too have adopted the "Cravath pay scale." Young lawyers live for bonuses and the legal press trumpets the results—but the news is all the same.

Each year, BigLaw shares a small fraction of its spoils to encourage its associates to stick around in spite of their misery and/or to entice law students to join their firm with the promise of bonuses. In fact, year-end bonuses are so common that associates typically await their year-end bonus before leaving a BigLaw job.

Plaintiffs' firms often offer better bonuses. But many still use the same flawed approach, which is often an "eat what you kill" model. If you work on a big case that hits, you get a big payout. If you don't work on the case that hits, you get left out.

That might sound fair. But it creates all the wrong incentives.

"Eat what you kill" discourages teamwork. Associates avoid helping on cases they're not staffed on. They jockey for position on the biggest cases or try to attach themselves to the best rainmakers. It turns the firm into a competition, when it should be a collaboration.

We rejected that model from day one.

Our approach is different. When the firm wins, everyone wins. Our system rewards results, not time. And it includes *everyone*, not just the lawyers. The IT guy, the legal assistants, the receptionist, and our barista all get bonuses too. Because we are all one team and everyone contributes to our success.

When we land a big success fee, we distribute bonuses immediately. We don't wait for year-end. We pay out in real time, when the success happens, so everyone shares in the moment and feels the reward. By paying bonuses to everyone in real time we are better able to build up the team and to reward and encourage collaboration.

We also believe in financial transparency. Every quarter, we share our firm's financial performance with all our lawyers, including our first-year lawyers. We believe in our model. We believe our people deserve to understand how the business works.

And unlike most firms, we don't hide the numbers.

CHAPTER 20

Our First Big Chance at a National Calling Card: Credit Suisse

O NE OF THE CASES THAT LANDED US on the national stage was a case we tried against Credit Suisse, one of the world's biggest banks at the time. They had an extensive history of dealing with crooks, money launderers, and corrupt politicians. They were even rumored to have laundered money for the Vatican.

We won an initial $40 million jury verdict for our client, Claymore Holdings, against Credit Suisse for fraud in 2014. We won a subsequent bench trial on certain additional nonjury claims in 2015, which expanded the award to nearly $287 million.

After seven years of litigation, the Texas State Supreme Court remanded the case to the trial court in 2020 solely to reconsider its damages award. In doing this, it did something it almost never does. The court usually tries to undo every jury verdict for fraud, but this time it let the jury's fraud verdict stand.

In June of 2021, on remand, the trial court awarded the plaintiffs $121 million. After a second remand and a new judgment for $64 million, the third round of appeals began in 2024. Credit Suisse has still not paid a penny. Although it has paid over $10 billion in fines and penalties since 2000 in forty-nine other legal cases, it is still fighting ours.

The Credit Suisse case is almost as old as Reid Collins. It began with a hunch by our client's general counsel, Scott Ellington, that Credit Suisse had a role in a busted loan on a big real estate deal called Lake Las Vegas. The $540 million loan was not supported by the value of the collateral underlying the loan. After a bankruptcy, the lenders received only $17 million for the collateral, but the appraisal supporting the loan stated that the value of that same collateral was between $511 million and $891 million.

That was 2007. A year later the markets fell off a cliff. Real estate took a nosedive, so it was not immediately obvious that there was malfeasance at the root of these large losses. Other lawyers told Ellington, "There's nothing here."

When he came to us, some of our team agreed. However, some of us wondered how half a billion dollars of collateral could be worth only $17 million, and we began to investigate the deal. It took us thousands of hours before we finally confirmed that this was not a story of real estate market losses. It was a story of misdeeds. Simply put, it was fraud committed by the investment bankers at Credit Suisse.

We had no proof of Credit Suisse's involvement because a lender in a loan syndicate like Claymore receives only the final appraisal ostensibly prepared by the appraiser. In order to understand Credit Suisse's involvement in the process that led to the appraisal, we had to get discovery from them.

Our job was to find out about that process, so we began with a case against CBRE, the appraisal firm. We sought discovery to understand what communications occurred between CBRE and the Credit Suisse investment bankers. Credit Suisse argued, "Your beef is with the appraiser, not us. What relevance does anything we did have with your case against the appraiser?" Our response was that they were integral to the process—Credit Suisse hired the appraiser and delivered the appraisal to the lenders. We need to know what role they played.

Our motive was to determine if we could prove that Credit Suisse played a hand in what seemed like a fraudulent appraisal. It was therefore critical that we get access to the key documents, which were the communications between Credit Suisse and the CBRE appraisers. That is why defendants fight tooth and nail not to give over their emails because, generally speaking, the goods are there. We had to file a motion to force them to turn the documents over and the judge said, "These documents are relevant. You need to turn them over."

We found that over the course of one weekend in April 2007, as they were preparing to market a $540 million refinancing loan, a group of Credit Suisse bankers and the appraiser conspired to pump up the values in the appraisal. In fact, one of the Credit Suisse bankers noticed a several-hundred-million-dollar error and wrote an email to her colleagues stating, "Let's maintain ignorance of it." The investment bankers mandated the appraisal results and pushed the value of the appraisal up by hundreds of millions of dollars.

We also found that in early 2004, the borrower had obtained an appraisal of about $220 million for the same property from the same appraiser. Approximately eight months later, using a redefined methodology dubbed the "total net value" method, Credit Suisse was able to generate an appraised value of over $1 billion in connection with the initial loan on the property, which was the same loan being refinanced in 2007.

No one would ever have known any of this if it were not for the system in which we can go into court, lay out our claim, and get access to documents that show what really happened. The jury found the facts compelling and ultimately found that Credit Suisse had committed fraud.

Many law firms would never handle a case like Credit Suisse, particularly not at the start, before we found the evidence we ultimately used to prove fraud. Very few firms would have taken the risk. We had to prove that the Credit Suisse investment bankers knowingly acted to inflate the value of the appraisal with the intention that it would be relied upon by our clients, who initially put in $250 million of the refi.

Why would a bank engage in blatant fraud? The fee. On a $540 million loan, the investment bank gets 2 percent: $10.8 million. The bankers were solely motivated by their year-end bonus to put money in their own pockets. They didn't care what happened as a consequence.

One of the senior bankers admitted there were problems with the appraisal and testified to many other things that damaged their case. He did not care. He lives in Connecticut, has a helicopter landing pad outside his house, and makes tens of millions of dollars a year at the bank. After trial, when he left the witness stand, he walked over to our table out of the presence of the jury, shook my hand, and said, "Good luck," with a smug look on his face.

The outcome didn't concern him at all.

The best lawyer in the world can't do anything without a client

I had initially met my client Scott Ellington while working at my former firm. We stayed in touch. In February of 2010, Scott called me at a hotel in Dubai and asked if we could sue Credit Suisse in a $540 million dollar case. He liked me and wanted to give me the chance, but told me without a bigger firm to assist, he probably couldn't convince his boss to hire my firm.

As luck would have it, soon after I formed my new firm, Marc Dworsky, a former adversary from a legal malpractice case, had reached out and offered me encouragement. He told me he'd like to find a case to work on together and complimented my team.

I reached out to Munger Tolles … and I now had the answer to Scott's question. Munger Tolles partnered with my firm in their first-ever contingency fee case.

Today, Marc is my partner.

Chapter 21:

Finding a Focus: Legal Malpractice

ONE OF THE REASONS OUR FIRM IS SO SUCCESSFUL is that we will do something that almost no other firm will do: We sue lawyers, even the biggest and most powerful BigLaw firms, for legal malpractice.

We have sued dozens of the top two hundred BigLaw firms for legal malpractice. Although it is only about 20 percent of our practice, pursuing claims against law firms is among the most interesting and rewarding work that we do.

We follow in a long line of law firms that have grown by following a maverick path. Weil Gotshal began as the only firm willing to do bankruptcy cases. Skadden Arps was the only firm willing to do mergers and acquisitions. Having a unique niche beats the alternative, which is being one of thousands of lawyers all willing to do the same work. For example, hourly fee defense work.

Most lawyers are reluctant to pursue claims against law firms. Many of them think that suing a law firm is "bad for business." Some lawyers think suing another lawyer is somehow distasteful or, worse, something only sleazy lawyers would do. I find the cases interesting—and, importantly, because few other quality firms are willing to pursue these claims, we enjoy a natural monopoly.

Meanwhile, I believe in holding everyone accountable for their actions—even fellow attorneys. No one has any problems suing accountants or bankers who do something wrong. I don't see why lawyers should be treated any differently.

I FIGHT BULLIES, AND PLENTY OF LAWYERS ARE BULLIES.

Of course, because individual lawyers occasionally do bad things does not make the whole profession bad, or even a whole firm. It does not even mean the individual is bad. Maybe they just made a mistake. But if they did, they should still be held accountable.

I am not sure why people think lawyers are special. Perhaps many lawyers are so concerned with generating new business that they feel preserving good relations with other law firms will help them gather referrals. Meanwhile, the majority of lawyers who think that way are all hourly fee lawyers at BigLaw. And let's be clear, they are all in competition with one another. They all do basically the same thing. So, believing that referrals will come from people who are in direct competition with you is foolish. How often are your competitors going to send you cases?

Perhaps it is some kind of misplaced professional courtesy. (I do know one thing: If you think lawyers are reluctant to sue other lawyers because they are worried about going up against brilliant legal minds . . . think again.)

Rather than drying up business because I broke some kind of lawyers' "code" by suing law firms, it actually *drove business to me*. Clients that initially came for legal malpractice saw how good my team was and used us for other things.

It opened doors for our firm rather than closing them. I frequently get calls from potential clients who say, "BigLaw firm XX gave me your name and said you are the person to talk to about suing a law firm," or "A lawyer who made me promise not to reveal their identity sent me your name because they previously defended one of your legal malpractice claims."

My favorite referrals are from former law firms that I have pursued claims against, their insurers, or the defense lawyers who defended them.

If you handle legal malpractice claims professionally, they essentially become an insurance matter. To us, it is not personal, it's just our business. We selectively choose our cases, so if we are suing a law firm, we strongly believe that we have a good faith basis. The reality is that, if we do not pursue a viable claim, it is almost certain that someone else will. And maybe another lawyer would not handle it as professionally as us or work so hard to resolve it on a pre-suit basis.

We have picked up a lot of dos and don'ts from our experience with legal malpractice.

What it's like to sue a
law firm ... twice

When I became a plaintiffs' lawyer, my North Star was that I like standing up for underdogs. That was one reason I enjoyed representing Alex van der Zwaan; another was that it allowed me to go up against one of my preferred adversaries: one of the most powerful law firms in the world.

Alex emailed me in early 2018 and said, "If you don't know me, just Google my name." I read the papers, so I knew his name. He was one of the first people to plead guilty in the Mueller investigation into Russian interference in the 2016 presidential election. Then he asked one of my favorite questions: "Would you be willing to sue my former firm?"

Alex was a lawyer at a large international law firm in London who, as a native Russian speaker, was tasked with helping his senior partners and Republican operatives Paul Manafort and Rick Gates to draft what later became known as the Tymoshenko Report.

Yulia Tymoshenko is the former prime minister of Ukraine who was imprisoned by the Yanukovych government after a six-week trial in a kangaroo court. Tymoshenko's lawyer was kicked out of court after the first week. She was eventually imprisoned for a lengthy sentence.

When Western politicians like US Secretary of State Hillary Clinton got upset, Yanukovych needed cover for Tymoshenko's continued imprisonment.

Alex went to Ukraine to talk to the witnesses and gather evidence to write a "report" validating the Tymoshenko prosecution. In the report, Alex and a team of lawyers from his firm concluded that, while the Tymoshenko trial had not met Western standards of due process, there had been at least some due process. The Yanukovych government then posted the Tymoshenko report on the Ukrainian government's website and used it as continued justification to keep Tymoshenko in prison.

When the Mueller investigation started looking at possible foreign interference in the 2016 presidential election, they subpoenaed Alex to ask him about his role in creating the report. More importantly, the Mueller team wanted to know about their dealings with Manafort and Gates, who were ultimately convicted for corruption in unrelated matters.

Alex did not know the US criminal process, but his employer told him, "Don't worry. We're going to represent you for free." He said, "OK. I didn't do anything wrong so I have nothing to worry about."

Alex came to the United States and spent eight hours being interviewed by an aggressive prosecutor named Andrew Weissmann, who was the second in charge of the Mueller team. Alex was "defended" by a lawyer at his firm. But because he was still a lawyer at the firm at the time, he was more concerned with saying anything that would jeopardize his job than in hiding anything from the government.

At one stage, the FBI asked Alex if he had met with Paul Manafort or Rick Gates after August of 2016, given that the election was in November of 2016. Alex replied, "Not that I can recall."

However, when he got back to his office in London he found tapes of discussions between him and a senior partner at his firm that showed he had talked to Manafort and Gates in September and October 2016.

Alex was not concerned with the government learning about the substance of what was on the tapes. But what worried him was that the recording could lead to his termination. On the tape, Alex had recorded his senior partner and some of the instructions he had given him on the Tymoshenko work. Because recording a senior partner at his firm would not have been received well, Alex had answered Weissmann's question with a "not that I can recall."

But when Alex returned to London, he felt remorse about his answer. He wanted to "do the right thing" and set the record straight. He called up "his" lawyer inside the firm and disclosed that he had tapes that indicated his answer was untruthful. His firm began an immediate investigation into the content of the tapes.

Of course, they had agreed to represent Alex and to be his lawyer. But rather than protect Alex and look out for his interests, they told Alex to hand over the tapes to the head of the London office and get on the next flight to New York.

If, instead of asking Alex to fly to New York, they had contacted the DOJ and negotiated a handover of the tapes, the matter would have been over quickly and easily. The DOJ was never going to extradite a guy from London to the US for saying, "Not that I can recall."

Instead of protecting Alex, they instructed him to come to the US. By doing so, they gave up all of Alex's leverage, which was the fact that he was outside of the DOJ's jurisdiction.

His employer, acting as his counsel, then turned over the tapes to the DOJ. They did so knowing that the tapes would reveal that Alex had lied when he said, "I don't know." But Alex had a Fifth Amendment right not to produce the tapes under the "act of production doctrine." Alex's employer never informed him of this right.

The DOJ then charged Alex with lying to a federal agent, which is a serious felony. This left Alex in real trouble. His wife was pregnant with their first child and he was stuck in the US until his case was over.

In March of 2018, when I met Alex for the first time, he was living in a Washington, DC, hotel room. He was stuck in the US and could not get his passport back until his criminal case was over. Soon thereafter, he pleaded guilty and received a thirty-day prison sentence. But then he had to wait five months for a prison assignment before he could serve his sentence. In effect, he was a prisoner in a foreign country for almost six months.

During that time, we made a client file demand upon Alex's law firm, seeking Alex's client file.

With the client file, It took several months to put the story together. Even thinking about it now, many years later, still enrages me.

We eventually reached out to Alex's law firm and offered to engage in a business discussion aimed at resolving Alex's claims. We shared a juicy, detailed complaint with them that we knew they would never let us file. In it, we contended that the law firm had a conflict of interest and breached their fiduciary duty to Alex. We included all of the details about how they represented themselves and Alex. But they had essentially abandoned Alex's interests in favor of their own.

The law firm later agreed to a confidential settlement.

The story gets even better.

The second lawsuit

A few months later, Tymoshenko's people called me up and said, "We're mad about this report. We want to sue this big international law firm." This was in late 2018. I responded, "I am very familiar with them."

Tymoshenko was the victim of a politically motivated prosecution orchestrated by Ukrainian President Viktor Yanukovych and his regime. After narrowly losing the 2010 presidential election, Tymoshenko was targeted through fabricated criminal charges relating to a 2009 gas deal she had negotiated with Russia.

Her 2011 trial was a sham: She was denied legal counsel, barred from calling witnesses, and prosecuted before a handpicked, inexperienced judge under the regime's control. Tymoshenko was convicted and sentenced to seven years in prison in proceedings widely condemned by the international community as violations of even basic due process and human rights.

To counter growing international pressure, Yanukovych—assisted by US lobbyist

Paul Manafort—retained a law firm to produce a report falsely validating Tymoshenko's conviction as legitimate and untainted by political bias (the same report that Alex had authored).

Although publicly framed as "independent," the report was secretly funded through millions of dollars funneled via offshore accounts controlled by Manafort. The firm not only whitewashed the proceedings but also assisted Ukrainian prosecutors and participated in lobbying efforts to legitimize Tymoshenko's imprisonment in the eyes of the West.

In 2013, the European Court of Human Rights found that Tymoshenko's imprisonment violated Articles 5 and 18 of the European Convention on Human Rights, concluding her imprisonment served political, not legal, ends. After the 2014 Euromaidan revolution and Yanukovych's flight to Russia (along with the trial judge who oversaw Tymoshenko's prosecution), Tymoshenko was finally released.

The new Ukrainian government admitted that her prosecution was politically motivated and acknowledged widespread human rights violations, including mistreatment in custody. The firm's role in facilitating and legitimizing this abuse became the subject of litigation and investigation in both Ukraine and the United States.

Tymoshenko was horribly treated by the Ukrainian authorities during her multiyear imprisonment. She was in a prison cell in which every square inch was under video surveillance. During her imprisonment she needed back surgery to remedy serious problems she was having. Rather than getting treatment from her own doctor, she was forced to use the prison doctor.

When she was finally released from prison in 2014, Tymoshenko was unable to walk. She literally left prison in a wheelchair.

Upon meeting Tymoshenko in December 2018, I was inspired by her courage. She told me that she was aware well in advance of her prosecution that the Yanukovych regime intended to prosecute her for political reasons. She could easily have left for Paris or elsewhere beyond Yanukovych's reach and waited out his term. But instead, she chose to stand up to him and face his prosecution.

At the conclusion of our initial meeting, I was sympathetic to her story but skeptical of her legal position. I told her, "No statute of limitations that I know of reaches back that far. The law firm did not act as your lawyer." I concluded, "I will take a look at this—but honestly, I am not sure that there is a claim here."

I gave the case to Josh Bruckerhoff, one of the young associates who had agreed to join Reid Collins on day one. At the firm, we call him "The Assassin" because of his remarkable ability to identify claims where others could not. I told him, "I don't know if there's anything to it, but let's see what you can come up with."

After a few days he came back with a grin and said, "I think we got something." I could not quite believe it. I said, "What claim could she possibly have after all of these years?" He said, "The Alien Tort Statute." I said, "You've got to be kidding me. Isn't that for pirates and stuff?" He said, "Yes." I asked, "Isn't it for government conduct?" He said, "Yes, but we have government conduct because the Yanukovych government are the people who wrongfully tried and convicted Tymoshenko."

I asked him, "Does the Alien Tort Statute have aiding and abetting liability so you can bring a claim against a private actor?" He said, "A two to one decision in the DC Court of Appeals says yes, there's aiding and abetting liability under the Alien Tort Statute."

I said, "What's the statute of limitations? This was seven years ago." The Assassin got a gleam in his eye. He paused for effect and said glibly, "Ten years." I responded, "You have got to be fucking kidding me."

I got to call up the same law firm and say, "Guess what? It's me again."

We used The Assassin's strategy to win a confidential settlement for Yulia Tymoshenko.

This is why developing a niche practice, especially one that has few competitors, in plaintiffs' law can be so rewarding.

Most lawyers won't sue lawyers. We will. Because we will, we get all sorts of interesting opportunities.

PART 5:

How to Start in Plaintiffs' Law

Chapter 22

How to Pick a Law Firm

If you don't choose a firm, a choice will be made for you

As a young lawyer, it is on you to choose a firm that has good finances and a good business model and that is not hiring rejects from other firms. As the legal industry becomes more unstable, it will only become more important to avoid firms with weak business models.

If you're going to commit to putting in the years of work that might eventually earn you a partnership, you are taking a big gamble on that firm being financially healthy. Do not be afraid to ask probing questions about the business model and about how it relates to you as an individual.

If the firm is right for you, they will be impressed by your due diligence and will give you honest answers. If they get pissed and refuse to engage with your questions, it's probably because they don't want you to hear the answers.

If you are considering joining a firm as an associate, some good questions about a firm's business model are:

- How do you finance your operations?
- Do you have any debt?
  - If so, what's the reasoning behind the debt?
- What is your business model?

- Can you explain it to me?
- How do you charge your clients (are you a pure hourly fee firm or do you utilize alternative billing structures)?
- Who are your major clients?
  - Are there just a few?
  - Are they concentrated in a few industries?
- Do you have any niche practices for which you have a competitive advantage?
- How do you plan to integrate artificial intelligence into your practice?
- How is work assigned?
  - Are you "dedicated" to an individual partner or group?
- Is there a mentor program?
- What formal training can you expect to receive?
  - For example, are you allowed to attend NITA (or other trial advocacy programs)?
- How are compensation and bonus decisions made?
- Who makes the compensation and bonus decisions?
- Are those people accessible?
- What office do they work in?
- Who makes the decision to promote lawyers to partner?
  - Are those people accessible?
  - Are they in the office you intend to work at?
- What percentage of your incoming associate class makes equity partner?
- Would you describe your firm as more lockstep or meritocracy?

You need to know the answers to these questions in order to gain a basic understanding of the law firm's business and its strengths and weaknesses. Equally important, you need to understand the firm's power structure, who makes the decisions that matter, and how those decisions are made.

ARE THE PEOPLE IN POWER AT THE FIRM GOING TO BE ACCESSIBLE TO YOU OR WILL THEY BE IN SOME REMOTE OFFICE?

The best advice that I can give in terms of interviewing for any legal job is to talk to the people three to five years ahead of you. Ask them what their work is like, whether the firm is well managed, and whether they understand the firm's business model. If you like the answers to those questions and the people you speak with are on a path that you can see yourself on, then maybe the firm is right for you.

If the lawyers a few years ahead of you are not on a path you would like to be on, are not getting meaningful work, and have little sense for the firm's business model and plan, then the firm is not likely to provide you with a better path. So you should look elsewhere.

You also need to assess a firm's client base to determine if it is too concentrated or industry-specific. Likewise, it is good to know what niche practices (if any) a firm has to make a determination if those practices are likely to thrive in the future or if they are subject to politics.

Think about it this way—if a firm lacks a true niche and is just offering an hourly fee service, then it faces enormous competition. If it serves a small client base or concentrated industry, then is that business subject to economic or political headwinds, or is it likely sustainable regardless of the economy or politics?

And again, the forced efficiency that artificial intelligence will bring to the legal industry must be thought through. If a given firm seems likely to benefit from efficiency, then it may be a better option than a firm that seems to rely exclusively on the billable hour. In general, smaller firms that charge some form of alternative fee seem destined to benefit from the enhanced efficiencies available through artificial intelligence. But it is worth asking the question of even hourly firms to see if they have a thoughtful answer.

But perhaps the most important factor in choosing any firm is culture. Are the people working at the firm your people? By "your people," I mean folks that you enjoy being around. I cannot emphasize this enough. If you are joining a firm that lacks a culture you can relate to, then you are very likely to be unhappy.

The law business is a people business. You have to like the people you are working with, or you'll be miserable.

Don't judge a firm by the art in the lobby. Judge them by the answers to your questions.

Jason Collins had been an auditor at Arthur Andersen before he went to law school. When he joined my former firm straight out of law school, he was focused on understanding the firm's financial situation. Of course, he watched (as many others did) as his former accounting firm imploded over allegations of wrongdoing in connection with its Enron work. Arthur Andersen was huge. No one ever thought it could go out of business. Jason realized any professional firm could disappear overnight. The fact that he had dodged a bullet by leaving for law school was just luck. And Jason did not want to rely on luck again.

As a law student who worked for the firm over two summers, he was able to take a critical look at the law firm's business model. One of the firm's primary practice areas was representing bankruptcy trustees, offshore liquidators, and SEC receivers, all of which are in the business of being plaintiffs. Jason asked himself, *What corporate plaintiff or what hedge fund that invests in litigation strategies could suffer repeated large losses for which it would need to pursue litigation and yet continue as a viable entity for any period of time?*

He argued that it would be tough for a regular company to continue to lose hundreds of millions of dollars on a regular basis due to wrongdoing and remain a functioning company. To Jason, representing professional plaintiffs like trustees and liquidators seemed like a good business model that he did not see many other law firms sharing. He liked the niche practice and the business plan.

Next, Jason did something that might have offended many would-be employers. He went to each partner in the firm and asked them, "Where do you get your business from?" and "How do you fit into the firm?" He also asked to see the firm's financial statements. Jason had seen Arthur Andersen go up in smoke and Enron collapse, so he asked critical questions about the firm's finances and borrowings to satisfy himself that he was getting into an enterprise that was well run, not just in terms of business strategy, but also from a financial standpoint.

He approached his potential employer in the same way that someone conducting due diligence to buy a company would.

I was working there at the time, and as an employer, I remember being impressed on a number of levels. He was asking questions that I would have been reluctant to ask at that stage of my career. And in some cases, he asked questions that I would never have thought to ask. I suspect that a number of my former partners had never thought to ask any of those questions either. For my own part, I had never even thought about professional plaintiff bankruptcy trustees in the way that Jason thought about it.

A decade later, Jason helped found Reid Collins with me and Lisa Tsai, before he retired at the age of forty-four.

Many years later, my good friend Alex Shoghi at the hedge fund Oasis, on whose behalf we brought the case against Renren that was one of our biggest successes, told me, "You guys are like a hedge fund. If a law firm was a hedge fund, it would be Reid Collins."

When I asked him what he meant, he said, "At Oasis, we spend time deciding whether or not a particular investment thesis warrants our investment dollars. At Reid Collins, you put the same effort into deciding whether to invest your human capital in a case as I do deciding whether to invest my money. So I think of you as a hedge fund operating as a law firm."

No one at law school encourages students to consider the legal industry in pure business terms—business strategy, strength of business, financial arrangements. Perhaps this contributes to the reticence of a lot of young lawyers to ask these questions.

Part of their hesitation is clearly fear that they will offend someone. Their attitude is often, "I want the job, so I shouldn't ask the question." But there is also a lack of business knowledge on the part of young lawyers, and that likely contributes to the problem because they don't even know which questions to ask.

TAKE IT FROM ME: ASKING THE HARD, BUT FAIR, QUESTIONS IS THE ONLY WAY TO PICK THE RIGHT FIRM.

Asking critical questions shows that you are not just willing to accept what seems to be a great plan without asking about it. It also demonstrates that you have the right kind of curiosity to be a good lawyer.

And you want to know the answers to these questions.

When evaluating a firm, the key is not to assume that their finances or client base are sound. Do your own homework to assure yourself that the firm you are thinking of joining has a sound financial footing and a solid client base. Do not be frightened to ask hard questions of any prospective employer.

CHAPTER 23

How to Actually Get a Plaintiffs' Job

B Y NOW, YOU KNOW THE CASE I'M MAKING: Plaintiffs' law is where you can find purpose and prosperity. It's where you get to choose your battles, work on cases that matter, and build a career you want.

But how do you actually get a plaintiffs' job?

Unlike BigLaw, there's no conveyor belt. There's no formal OCI process. There's no easy path into the firms.

Plaintiffs' firms are often smaller and far less focused on hiring for hiring's sake. They don't always post openings. Some may require that you take less salary than the BigLaw path.

So here's the truth: You have to go find them and make them see why you're worth a shot. You may have to sacrifice some starting salary in order to get experience.

You must identify firms that fit you

Not all plaintiffs' firms are created equal. Some do personal injury work. Some do mass torts. Some focus on consumer protection, employment discrimination, whistleblower claims, investor fraud, or complex financial litigation, like we do at my firm.

You need to figure out which kind of plaintiffs' work excites you. Of course, this starts with figuring out what subject matter excites you. But an important component is focusing on where you think you can have the most impact that will matter to you. Then you can begin to look at:

- Where do you want to live and which firm(s) are in the area?
- Who's winning big cases?
- Where are your kind of people working?
- Which firms in your area are filing the types of cases that excite you?
- Which firms are regularly in court?

The best alternative to OCI

The single best alternative to OCI is clear and simple. Join the NPLA and participate in your school's PLA.

The National Plaintiffs' Law Association (NPLA) was created for people like you— law students and young lawyers who are serious about a career in plaintiffs' law. The NPLA runs events, provides resources, teaches you about various avenues available to plaintiffs' lawyers, and most importantly, *helps connect you with actual opportunities.*

Every year, the NPLA hosts a job fair specifically for plaintiffs' firms. It's one of the few structured settings where plaintiffs' firms actually recruit. Make it a priority to attend.

And if your school doesn't yet have a local PLA chapter, then start one. These student groups are an incredible way to build relationships, invite plaintiffs' lawyers to speak, and put yourself on the radar of firms that don't usually show up on campus.

Joining or starting a PLA chapter sends a clear signal: *I'm not following the herd.* Most importantly, it is the best alternative to OCI that I am aware of where you can find non-BigLaw jobs.

Once you have identified a firm, follow up or reach out the right way

If you met a firm at the NPLA job fair, then you've already cleared the hardest hurdle: *You got in the room.* Now your job is to stand out from the other candidates. That means follow-up.

Send a short, direct email to the lawyer you spoke with (or someone you were introduced to):

- Reference your prior meeting;
- Thank them for their time;
- Say something thoughtful about what you learned from them; and
- Make it clear you're still very interested in their work and want to be part of their team.

Keep it real. Keep it brief. And send it within a few days of the event. This isn't networking theater, it's about staying on their radar.

If you didn't meet them at the job fair, and you're reaching out cold, then treat your outreach differently. No mass emails. No "To whom it may concern." You're applying to a firm that fights battles. You need to show them you know how to pick one.

Write a sharp, direct email, to a specific person:

- Show that you've researched the firm's work as well as the lawyer's work;
- Try to identify something you share in common (e.g., you went to the same school, grew up in the same town, etc.);
- Tell them *why* you're reaching out;
- Make it clear that you want to do the kind of work that the firm is doing; and
- Keep it short. Keep it real.

Whether it's follow-up or first contact, the same rule applies: *You're trying to connect. Not just apply.*

Try it before you buy it

Once you have narrowed your focus to a few areas of law that interest you, then go try them out. The only way to really know if a career path is for you is to actually *do* the work. It is very helpful to see as many firms as you can before you pick one to start at.

And once you've sampled a firm, compared it to others, and know it could sustain you, take a close look at all of the things that we have covered in this book. Does the firm have a good business model? Is it well managed? Are people three to five years ahead of you on the path that you want to be on?

Most important of all: Are these "your people"?

Once you get an opportunity, show you want it

Once you get an opportunity, don't just do what you're asked. You need to go the extra mile. I refer to this as "the entrepreneurial associate."

The ideal associate is the one who looks beyond the assigned task they're given. They figure out just how this task fits into the bigger mission. Once you understand how a given task fits into the bigger mission, then do what you're asked *and* add to the assigned work as an entrepreneur would.

In other words, move the case forward as a teammate would, not as a robot. See if there are other things that would provide a better solution to the problem assigned to you ... *and go do them.*

This kind of entrepreneurial hustle turns heads. It's how a lot of the best people I know got ahead in the legal business through hard work. A very successful friend of mind likes to tell young people, the one thing no one can take from you is hard work. Just showing up early and working hard goes a long way. Frankly, if you're passionate about the work, then it's a lot easier to work hard.

Be aggressive about getting experience

No matter where you go, you will need to be aggressive to get experience. Hopefully, you have chosen a firm that trains up its team and you will get on-the-job training. Remember, plaintiffs' law rewards skills—not credentials. If you can try a case and you're comfortable on your feet someone will want to hire you.

But it can be more basic than that. Do not wait for work to come to you. You must go seek out the type of work that will get you the experience you need. If your firm brings in a case that interests you, go find the partner whose case it is and lobby to be on the team. Trust me, showing interest will set you apart.

And as for getting trial experience, you will need to get creative. Consider trial advocacy training at a place like NITA, try getting pro bono work, consider a stint as a local prosecutor, but most importantly *beg, borrow, or steal to get on any team going to trial wherever you are.*

You must build, grow, and nurture your network

One of the great advantages of plaintiffs' law is that you stand out. Most of your peers from law school won't be doing what you are doing. That means your peer network from law school can help refer you business, but only if you stay in contact with them.

Be strategic about growing your network. Depending on your niche, different contacts will matter more. But across the board, remember: Networks are like plants. They need water. Help people in your network. Don't just look for what they can give you.

Stay in contact, follow up, and make it fun.

The final word on a job hunt for a plaintiffs' job

If you're waiting for a job posting or a perfect path, stop. That's not how this world works. You're going to have to go off-road. Sure, you should attend the NPLA job fair, but this is likely going to require more effort than attending OCI and signing up to meet a couple of firms. The jobs you will most want are the ones that will require some effort.

But here's the upside: The people who succeed in plaintiffs' law are the same people who were willing to bet on themselves. They are also the people most likely to find true purpose and reward in the law.

And if you've read this far, that's probably you.

Go get it.

CONCLUSION:

The Case for a Career in Plaintiffs' Law

L AW SCHOOL DOESN'T TEACH YOU how to build a meaningful legal career. To be fair, it was never intended to.

But the problem is that students don't know this. So they default into paths that look prestigious, feel safe, and often turn out to be neither.

BigLaw was never designed for you. It was designed to serve itself.

It's a machine built on hourly billing, burnout, and a revolving door of junior talent. And with the rise of AI, that machine is about to break down. The old model in which people ground it out for a decade, hoping to make partner, is collapsing. The artificial intelligence wave is coming.

There's a different path. One that law school barely mentions. One that doesn't rely on the billable hour or meaningless work representing bullies. That path is plaintiffs' law.

Plaintiffs' law is the path where you can find passion, purpose, and prosperity.

Most plaintiffs' firms are leaner and poised to harness AI's true potential. Rather than sitting in the path of the storm, plaintiffs' boutiques, like mine, are going to massively profit from AI.

Plaintiffs' lawyers will continue to choose their clients and their battles. They'll still pursue liars, thieves, frauds, and bullies and they will continue to have meaningful work. And they'll still love what they do. The difference? With AI, they will be hyperefficient at doing it.

So here's my advice:

Don't chase someone else's idea of success. Don't make career decisions based on fear, debt, or prestige.

Make them based on what kind of lawyer and what kind of person you actually want to be.

If you want true fulfillment in your legal career and you want a career that actually has a future, then I encourage you to pursue a career in plaintiffs' law.

And good luck.

Acknowledgments

I would never have even thought to write this book if it had not been for my good friend Tucker Max. Over a year ago, after I told him about an inspiring young law student named Julia—who figured out her path to becoming a plaintiffs' lawyer largely on her own—he said, "You need to write a book." That conversation planted the seed for this book.

This book wouldn't exist without the encouragement and feedback of a number of my friends, including Tucker, Clay Hebert, Lisa Blue, Brad Beckworth, Mark Lebovitch, Katrina Dewey, Marc Dworsky, Aaron Brown, Josh Bruckerhoff, Tom Washmon, Barbara Balliette, Tom Meredith, and Angel Fahy.

Thank you for helping me to say what I actually meant. I'm grateful for your time, honesty, and belief in the message.

I've been so fortunate over the course of my career. I truly love my profession and feel the need to give back in any way that I can. If this book helps anyone make better choices about their career, it's because of what my many mentors and friends taught me over the years. The mistakes are mine. The lessons are theirs.

About the Author

Bill Reid has accomplished what few other trial lawyers have: he has won jury trials in all four possible sides of litigation. He's tried (and won) cases as a federal prosecutor, a criminal defense lawyer, a plaintiffs' attorney in high-stakes civil cases, and a civil defense lawyer for major companies. He's seen how the system works from every angle—and how to win from each one.

He also knows law as a business. Bill founded Reid Collins & Tsai from scratch and, in under a decade, built it into a nationally recognized trial firm. That combination—courtroom success and entrepreneurial leadership—gives him a perspective few lawyers ever develop. He's worked in firms big and small, brought plaintiff-side cases and defended them, and built a practice that is both prosperous and rewarding.

At the University of Texas School of Law, he teaches Complex Financial Litigation, a practical course he created to teach students how to use their theory in the real world.

This book is adapted from one of the most popular modules in that class: "Advice I Wish I'd Received." It's everything he wishes someone had told him before starting his career.